I0703291

DECODING NEURO-LINGUISTIC PROGRAMMING

TOOLS FOR MORE EFFECTIVE COMMUNICATION

DAVID SANDUA

INDEX

I. INTRODUCTION

The world of communication is a complex and multifaceted realm, where understanding and interpreting the nuances of human interaction can make all the difference in our personal and professional lives. Neuro-Linguistic Programming (NLP) offers a unique set of tools and techniques that can revolutionize the way we approach communication, enabling us to decipher the underlying patterns and signals that shape our interactions. By delving into the intricacies of verbal and non-verbal cues, NLP equips individuals with the skills to establish stronger connections, foster trust, and influence others positively. Through the exploration of concepts like calibration, anchoring, and reframing, this book sheds light on how these principles can be harnessed to overcome communication barriers and achieve desired outcomes. With a focus on practical applications and real-world examples, readers are encouraged to reflect on their own communication styles and adopt a more mindful and effective approach to building relationships. This book serves as a comprehensive guide for anyone seeking to enhance their communicative abilities and unlock the full potential of their interpersonal interactions.

Definition of NLP

NLP can be defined as a psychological approach that focuses on the connection between neurology, language, and behavioral patterns. It involves understanding how individuals perceive the world through their senses, how they communicate both verbally and non-verbally, and how these aspects influence their behavior. NLP techniques aim to reprogram the way individuals think and react to stimuli by providing them with tools to effectively communicate, build rapport, and achieve personal growth. By delving into concepts such as calibration, anchoring, and reframing, individuals can learn to better understand themselves and others, leading to improved relationships and increased success in various aspects of their lives. Through the study and application of NLP, individuals can enhance their communication skills, boost their confidence, and ultimately, transform their lives for the better.

Overview of NLP's relevance to effective communication

In analyzing the relevance of NLP to effective communication, it becomes evident that NLP offers a unique toolkit that can significantly enhance one's ability to connect with others. By honing in on the subtle cues present in both verbal and non-verbal communication, individuals can develop a deeper understanding of people's perspectives and emotions. This heightened awareness allows for the establishment of stronger rapport and the ability to influence others positively. The techniques of calibration, anchoring, and reframing, extensively covered in NLP, provide practical ways to navigate communication barriers and achieve greater clarity and persuasiveness in interactions. Through real-life examples and case studies, the efficacy of NLP in various contexts, such as leadership, education, therapy, and personal relationships, is demonstrated. Ultimately, mastering NLP techniques not only leads to improved communication skills but also encourages individuals to reflect on their communication style and approach, fostering more mindful and effective interactions.

Objectives of the research essay

Furthermore, the objectives of the research essay delve deeper into the practical applications of NLP techniques in enhancing communication. By examining concepts such as calibration, anchoring, and reframing, the research aims to demonstrate how these tools can be utilized to decode and interpret both verbal and non-verbal signals effectively. Through case studies and examples showcasing the successful implementation of NLP in various fields, the research seeks to highlight the potential impact of NLP on improving interpersonal relationships and achieving desired outcomes. By uncovering the underlying principles of NLP and illustrating their real-world implications, the research essay aims to provide a comprehensive understanding of how NLP can be a powerful tool for enhancing communication skills and fostering meaningful connections. Ultimately, the research essay strives to empower readers to reflect on their own communication practices and adopt NLP strategies to navigate complex social interactions with confidence and effectiveness.

II. HISTORICAL DEVELOPMENT OF NLP

An essential aspect of understanding NLP is tracing its historical development. A pivotal moment in the evolution of NLP was the collaboration between Richard Bandler and John Grinder in the 1970s. Drawing inspiration from the work of renowned therapists such as Fritz Perls and Virginia Satir, Bandler and Grinder sought to discover the patterns of communication and behavior that lead to successful outcomes in therapy. Through their study and modeling of these individuals, they developed the foundational principles of NLP, emphasizing the connection between language, behavior, and subjective experience. This approach marked a paradigm shift in the field of psychology, as it offered a systematic framework for understanding and improving communication. As NLP continued to evolve, various techniques and concepts were refined and expanded upon, solidifying its reputation as a powerful tool for personal and professional growth.

Origins and founders of NLP

As NLP gained popularity in the 1970s, its origins can be traced back to the collaborative efforts of Richard Bandler and John Grinder. Bandler, a computer scientist, and Grinder, a linguistics professor, merged their expertise to create a model of human behavior that would revolutionize the field of communication. Drawing inspiration from renowned therapists such as Fritz Perls and Virginia Satir, the founders focused on studying successful patterns of behavior to understand how individuals can achieve their goals through effective communication. By analyzing the language, beliefs, and behavioral patterns of exceptional communicators, Bandler and Grinder formulated the foundational principles of NLP. Their innovative approach emphasized the power of language and perception in shaping our reality, paving the way for a new understanding of human communication and behavior. Through their pioneering work, Bandler and Grinder laid the groundwork for a transformative methodology that continues to empower individuals to enhance their communication skills and achieve personal growth.

Evolution of NLP over the decades

Over the decades, NLP has undergone a significant evolution, adapting to changing communication styles and technological advancements. Initially developed in the 1970s, NLP drew upon principles from psychology, linguistics, and computer science to create a system of understanding and influencing human behavior through language. As research in cognitive science and communication theory progressed, NLP techniques evolved to encompass a wider range of applications, from therapy and coaching to sales and leadership. The integration of Artificial Intelligence (AI) and machine learning in recent years has further expanded the possibilities of NLP, allowing for more sophisticated analysis of language patterns and communication dynamics. This progression has led to the development of specialized tools and algorithms that can assist individuals in interpreting and responding to verbal and non-verbal cues more effectively, ultimately enhancing their communication skills across diverse contexts.

Key milestones in NLP research

One of the key milestones in NLP research can be traced back to the work of Richard Bandler and John Grinder in the 1970s. Their collaboration led to the development of NLP as a practical methodology for understanding and modeling human behavior. Through the analysis of successful therapists such as Virginia Satir and Milton Erickson, Bandler and Grinder identified patterns of language, behavior, and thought that could be leveraged for personal growth and communication enhancement. This groundbreaking research laid the foundation for key NLP techniques such as the Meta Model and the Milton Model, which revolutionized the field by providing structured frameworks for analyzing and influencing communication dynamics. By identifying these fundamental patterns, Bandler and Grinder opened up new possibilities for individuals to achieve greater self-awareness and effectiveness in their interactions with others.

III. FUNDAMENTAL PRINCIPLES OF NLP

Another crucial aspect of NLP is the understanding of its fundamental principles. These principles serve as the foundation upon which all NLP techniques are built, guiding practitioners towards more effective communication strategies. One key principle is the concept of sensory acuity, which emphasizes the importance of being fully present and attentive to both verbal and non-verbal cues during interactions. By honing their sensory acuity skills, individuals can better calibrate their responses to match the communication styles of others, leading to improved rapport and understanding. Additionally, the principle of congruence underscores the significance of aligning one's thoughts, words, and actions to convey authenticity and credibility in communication. Overall, a deep understanding and application of these fundamental principles are essential for practitioners to harness the full power of NLP techniques in enhancing their communication skills and achieving their desired outcomes.

The presuppositions of NLP

In exploring the presuppositions of NLP , it becomes evident that the foundational beliefs underpinning this approach to communication are fundamental to its effectiveness. One key presupposition is the idea that individuals operate based on their subjective experience, meaning that perception shapes reality. This understanding encourages practitioners of NLP to approach communication with empathy and openness, recognizing that different perspectives can lead to different interpretations of the same situation. Another core presupposition is that communication is a two-way process, emphasizing the importance of both verbal and non-verbal cues in conveying messages effectively. By acknowledging these presuppositions and integrating them into practice, individuals can enhance their ability to establish rapport, build meaningful connections, and influence others positively through more nuanced and mindful communication strategies. Ultimately, embracing the presuppositions of NLP can lead to more profound insights into human interaction and pave the way for more effective communication in various contexts.

The communication model according to NLP

In understanding the communication model according to NLP, it is crucial to recognize the intricate interplay between language, neurology, and behavior. NLP posits that individuals perceive the world through their senses, and this perception shapes their internal representation of reality. Through linguistic processes, such as language patterns and metaphors, individuals create meaning and communicate their experiences. Neurologically, this communication model suggests that the brain processes information based on sensory inputs, filters, and stores them accordingly. Behavior, the final component of the model, encompasses how individuals act in response to their perceptions and linguistic interpretations. By comprehensively addressing these three elements, NLP offers a unique framework to enhance communication by identifying patterns, beliefs, and behaviors that may hinder effective interactions. It empowers individuals to reframe their perspectives, align their language with their intentions, and build rapport with others through heightened awareness and flexibility in communication strategies.

The concept of subjective experience

When considering the concept of subjective experience within the realm of NLP , it becomes apparent that individual perceptions play a crucial role in shaping communication dynamics. NLP emphasizes the importance of understanding subjective experiences, as every person interprets the world uniquely due to their past experiences, beliefs, and values. By acknowledging and respecting these subjective realities, communicators can tailor their messages more effectively to resonate with others on a deeper level. Furthermore, NLP techniques such as mirroring and matching can help bridge the gap between different subjective experiences, fostering greater empathy and connection. In essence, subjective experience acts as a lens through which individuals perceive and interpret the world, influencing their communication style and interactions with others. By incorporating the understanding of subjective experience into NLP practices, individuals can enhance their ability to communicate authentically and build meaningful relationships based on mutual understanding and respect.

IV. NLP AND PERCEPTION

One significant aspect of NLP is its influence on perception. NLP techniques are designed to enhance an individual's ability to perceive and interpret both verbal and non-verbal cues effectively. By understanding the nuances of communication, individuals can build stronger rapport with others and positively influence their interactions. Through practices such as calibration, anchoring, and reframing, individuals can fine-tune their perception and responses, leading to clearer and more persuasive communication. The application of these techniques in real-life scenarios, as demonstrated in the book, showcases the transformative power of NLP in overcoming communication barriers and achieving desired outcomes. By honing their perceptual skills through the principles of NLP, individuals can cultivate a more mindful and effective communication style, ultimately strengthening their interpersonal relationships and achieving success in various domains of life.

The role of sensory acuity

When it comes to understanding the nuances of effective communication, sensory acuity plays a crucial role in decoding the messages we receive from others. By sharpening our awareness of subtle cues such as tone of voice, body language, and facial expressions, individuals can gain deeper insights into the thoughts and emotions of those around them. In the context of NLP , sensory acuity serves as a foundation for building rapport, establishing trust, and influencing positive outcomes in interactions. By paying attention to the sensory signals being transmitted, practitioners of NLP can tune into the underlying meanings behind words and actions, leading to more authentic and impactful communication. Through honing sensory acuity skills, individuals can enhance their ability to connect with others on a deeper level, fostering understanding and fostering stronger relationships. In essence, sensory acuity is a powerful tool in the NLP toolkit that can elevate communication to a more profound and insightful level.

Filters of perception in NLP

The concept of filters of perception in NLP is essential for understanding how individuals interpret and process information in their interactions. These filters, including beliefs, values, past experiences, and emotional states, shape how people perceive the world around them and influence their communication style. By recognizing and understanding these filters, individuals can become more aware of their biases and limitations, allowing them to adjust their communication strategies accordingly. NLP provides techniques to help individuals navigate through these filters, such as meta-modeling, which encourages questioning and challenging assumptions, and sensory acuity, which heightens awareness of subtle cues. By effectively managing these filters of perception, individuals can enhance their communication skills, build stronger connections with others, and achieve more meaningful outcomes in their personal and professional relationships. Ultimately, mastering the understanding and manipulation of these filters can lead to more effective and successful communication in all aspects of life.

How NLP suggests perception shapes communication

In the realm of NLP , the intricate relationship between perception and communication is a central focus. NLP suggests that our perceptions of the world around us significantly impact how we communicate with others. By understanding how our own beliefs, values, and past experiences shape our perceptions, individuals can begin to grasp how these factors influence their interactions with others. Through NLP techniques such as mirroring, matching, and pacing, individuals can align their communication styles with those of their counterparts, fostering better understanding and rapport. Furthermore, NLP highlights the importance of adapting one's language patterns and non-verbal cues to effectively convey messages and establish connections with others. By honing in on how perception shapes communication, NLP offers a valuable framework for enhancing interpersonal relationships and achieving more effective communication outcomes.

V. REPRESENTATIONAL SYSTEMS

Understanding representational systems is crucial in NLP as they play a significant role in how individuals process information and communicate with others. Representational systems refer to the sensory modalities through which people perceive and interpret the world, including visual (seeing), auditory (hearing), kinesthetic (feeling), olfactory (smelling), and gustatory (tasting) channels. By recognizing and utilizing these systems, NLP practitioners can tailor their communication to better resonate with the recipient's preferred mode of processing. This alignment enhances rapport-building, facilitates understanding, and increases the effectiveness of the message being conveyed. Through techniques such as matching and mirroring, individuals can establish a deeper connection by aligning their representational systems with those of their counterparts. By incorporating an awareness of representational systems into their communication strategies, individuals can enhance their ability to connect with others and achieve more impactful outcomes in various aspects of their lives.

Visual, auditory, and kinesthetic systems

As communication is a multifaceted process, understanding the interconnectedness of the visual, auditory, and kinesthetic systems is crucial for effective interpersonal interactions. The visual system plays a significant role in processing non-verbal cues such as facial expressions, body language, and gestures, providing valuable insights into a person's emotional state and intentions. In contrast, the auditory system processes verbal information, including tone of voice, pitch, and speed of speech, which can greatly impact the meaning and reception of the message. Additionally, the kinesthetic system, which includes touch and physical movements, contributes to building rapport and creating connections through a sense of presence and engagement. By recognizing and utilizing these sensory systems in communication, individuals can enhance their ability to convey and interpret messages accurately, build stronger connections, and ultimately achieve more successful outcomes in their interactions. This integrated approach to communication, grounded in an understanding of visual, auditory, and kinesthetic systems, empowers individuals to navigate complex social dynamics with greater skill and confidence.

Identifying representational systems in communication

An essential aspect of understanding NLP lies in the identification of representational systems in communication. These systems, comprising visual, auditory, kinesthetic, olfactory, and gustatory elements, play a crucial role in how individuals process and interpret information. By recognizing and analyzing these systems, communicators can tailor their messages to resonate more effectively with others. For instance, a visually-oriented individual may respond more positively to vivid imagery, whereas an auditory-oriented person may prefer auditory cues. Understanding these preferences can lead to more impactful and persuasive communication, enabling individuals to establish stronger connections and influence outcomes. By honing the ability to identify and align with different representational systems, communicators can significantly enhance their communicative effectiveness across various contexts, ultimately fostering more meaningful and productive interactions.

Adapting communication styles to different systems

As individuals navigate through various systems and contexts, the ability to adapt communication styles becomes essential for effective interaction. In the realm of NLP , understanding and adjusting communication patterns to fit different environments is emphasized as a key component for successful outcomes. By recognizing the unique communication preferences and cues within diverse systems, individuals can tailor their approach to resonate more effectively with others. This adaptive process involves not only verbal articulation but also non-verbal signals, tone of voice, and body language. Through the application of NLP techniques such as pacing and leading, individuals can establish rapport and influence others positively. Ultimately, the mastery of adapting communication styles to different systems allows for smoother interactions, increased mutual understanding, and enhanced connections in both personal and professional settings.

VI. RAPPORT BUILDING TECHNIQUES IN NLP

One of the foundational pillars of NLP lies in the art of rapport building. By establishing a strong rapport with others, individuals can create a foundation of trust and connection that facilitates effective communication. In the realm of NLP, various techniques have been devised to enhance rapport building, including mirroring and matching, pacing and leading, and establishing rapport through linguistic techniques such as sensory-based language and presuppositions. These techniques are rooted in the understanding that establishing rapport is not merely about mirroring body language, but also about mirroring and matching the cognitive and emotional states of others. By aligning oneself with the internal experiences of others, individuals practicing NLP can create a sense of empathy and understanding that paves the way for more meaningful interactions and positive outcomes. In essence, rapport building techniques in NLP serve as a gateway to creating genuine connections and fostering productive relationships in both personal and professional settings.

The concept of mirroring and matching

One powerful concept within NLP is the idea of mirroring and matching. This technique involves subtly imitating the behaviors, speech patterns, and gestures of the person you are communicating with in order to create a sense of rapport and connection. By mirroring and matching, individuals can build trust and establish a deeper level of understanding with others. Through this process, unconscious rapport is established, allowing for smoother and more effective communication to take place. This technique can be particularly valuable in situations where building rapport quickly is essential, such as in negotiations, sales, or therapy sessions. Overall, mirroring and matching can be a powerful tool in enhancing communication effectiveness and fostering positive relationships in various contexts. The ability to mirror and match effectively can significantly impact one's ability to influence, persuade, and connect with others on a deeper level.

Pacing and leading techniques

By utilizing pacing and leading techniques within the context of NLP , individuals can effectively establish rapport and influence others in a positive manner. Pacing involves mirroring the verbal and non-verbal behavior of the person being communicated with, creating a sense of connection and understanding. This technique helps build trust and create a harmonious communication environment. Once rapport is established, the concept of leading can be introduced, where subtle shifts in language or behavior guide the conversation towards a desired outcome. By smoothly transitioning from pacing to leading, individuals can influence others' thoughts, emotions, and behaviors, ultimately fostering a more productive and impactful exchange. Through the strategic application of pacing and leading techniques, individuals can enhance their communication skills, build stronger relationships, and achieve success in various personal and professional endeavors.

Building rapport in different contexts

One crucial aspect of NLP lies in the ability to build rapport effectively in different contexts. Building rapport is not a one-size-fits-all approach; it requires a deep understanding of the nuances of communication and interpersonal dynamics. In professional settings, building rapport can enhance collaboration, trust, and teamwork among colleagues. Leaders who master the art of rapport-building can inspire and motivate their team members to achieve common goals. In personal relationships, rapport can foster deep connections, empathy, and mutual understanding. Understanding the unique needs and communication styles of individuals is key to establishing a strong rapport that withstands challenges and conflict. By utilizing NLP techniques such as mirroring, pacing, and leading, individuals can create authentic connections that lay the foundation for effective communication and positive influence in various contexts.

VII. META-MODELS IN NLP

One key aspect of NLP that has proven to be instrumental in enhancing communication is the use of meta-models. These models act as frameworks that help individuals better understand and interpret the meaning behind the words and behaviors of others. By uncovering and addressing the underlying structure of language patterns, meta-models allow for more precise communication and the ability to elicit clearer information from conversations. Meta-models in NLP provide a systematic approach to identifying and rectifying linguistic distortions, generalizations, and deletions that can hinder effective communication. They enable individuals to ask strategic questions to fill in missing information, challenge assumptions, and expand their understanding of the speaker's intended message. Overall, the incorporation of meta-models in NLP equips individuals with the tools necessary to decipher and respond to communication more effectively, fostering deeper connections and facilitating successful interactions.

Definition and purpose of the Meta-Model

One fundamental tool within NLP is the Meta-Model, which serves as a framework for understanding and challenging the language patterns that individuals use. The Meta-Model aims to clarify and expand the information presented in communication by questioning assumptions, generalizations, and distortions. By identifying and addressing these linguistic elements, individuals can improve the accuracy and specificity of their communication, leading to greater clarity and understanding in interactions. The purpose of the Meta-Model is to uncover hidden meanings, clarify misconceptions, and facilitate more effective communication between individuals. Through its structured approach to language analysis, the Meta-Model can help individuals become more aware of the nuances in communication and enhance their ability to express themselves clearly and accurately. Overall, the Meta-Model serves as a powerful tool for enhancing communication skills and fostering deeper connections with others in various contexts.

Techniques to clarify and specify communication

An integral aspect of NLP is the utilization of techniques that aim to clarify and specify communication in order to enhance understanding and facilitate effective interaction. By honing in on key concepts such as calibration, anchoring, and reframing, individuals can learn to decode subtle cues and nuances in communication, allowing for a more accurate grasp of intended messages. Through the practice of these techniques, individuals can bridge the gap between verbal and non-verbal communication, establishing a stronger rapport and connection with others. Moreover, by employing these tools, individuals can refine their own communication styles, adapt to different contexts, and ultimately achieve their communicative goals. NLP techniques not only empower individuals to decipher complex messages but also encourage self-reflection and a more intentional approach to interpersonal interactions, making them invaluable resources for those seeking to improve their communication skills and cultivate meaningful relationships.

Practical applications of the Meta-Model

The practical applications of the Meta-Model within NLP offer invaluable tools for enhancing communication effectiveness. By utilizing techniques such as calibration, anchoring, and reframing, individuals can decode the underlying structure of language and uncover hidden meanings in conversations. For professionals, this means being able to build rapport swiftly, identify and respond to clients' needs more effectively, and influence outcomes positively. In personal relationships, these tools can help foster better understanding, resolve conflicts, and cultivate deeper connections. Through case studies and real-life examples, it becomes evident how NLP techniques can be tailored to various contexts to overcome communication barriers and achieve desired outcomes. By integrating the Meta-Model into daily interactions, individuals can elevate their communication skills and create more meaningful and impactful relationships.

VIII. THE MILTON MODEL

The Milton Model, a key component of NLP , is a powerful language pattern developed by Dr. Milton Erickson. This model aims to induce trance-like states of focused attention and bypass critical faculties to access the unconscious mind. By utilizing linguistic structures such as embedded commands, analogical marking, and presuppositions, the Milton Model allows communicators to influence others subtly and effectively. This technique is particularly useful in therapeutic settings, coaching sessions, and negotiation scenarios where building rapport and influencing behavior are crucial. Through the use of vague language and storytelling, the Milton Model promotes open-ended communication that encourages listeners to fill in the gaps with their own interpretations, leading to deeper engagement and receptivity to suggestions. Overall, mastering the Milton Model can significantly enhance one's ability to communicate persuasively and build more meaningful connections with others.

Understanding the Milton Model

In the realm of NLP , the Milton Model stands out as a pivotal tool for enhancing communication effectiveness. Developed by renowned hypnotherapist Milton H. Erickson, this model focuses on language patterns and techniques that can subtly influence individuals' unconscious minds. By understanding the structure of language and its impact on the subconscious, practitioners of the Milton Model can establish rapport, create positive outcomes, and induce trance-like states for therapeutic purposes.

Through the utilization of linguistic patterns such as presuppositions, embedded commands, and ambiguous language, communicators can bypass conscious resistance and facilitate deeper connections with others. The Milton Model not only provides a framework for more impactful communication but also offers insights into human behavior and thought processes, making it a valuable asset for those seeking to improve their interpersonal skills and influence others effectively.

Techniques for influential and persuasive communication

As individuals strive to enhance their communication skills, it is crucial to delve into the techniques that can truly make an impact in influencing others. One such technique is the art of calibration, which involves keenly observing and interpreting verbal and non-verbal cues to better understand the person you are communicating with. This allows for a more personalized and tailored approach, leading to more effective interactions. Additionally, anchoring serves as a powerful tool in persuasive communication by associating certain emotions or feelings with specific stimuli, thereby influencing the individual's response. Furthermore, reframing provides a unique perspective on situations, enabling individuals to shift their mindset and approach challenges from a different angle. By mastering these techniques, individuals can not only improve their communication skills but also become more influential and persuasive in their interactions, ultimately leading to greater success in various aspects of life.

Differences between the Meta-Model and the Milton Model

One fundamental aspect of NLP is the understanding of the differences between the Meta-Model and the Milton Model. The Meta-Model focuses on challenging and clarifying the client's language, aiming to uncover hidden beliefs or assumptions. It is a more direct and structured approach, often used to bring awareness to distortions, generalizations, and deletions in communication. On the other hand, the Milton Model, named after the renowned psychotherapist Milton Erickson, takes a more indirect and permissive approach. This model is designed to bypass conscious resistance by utilizing vague language, presuppositions, and embedded commands to access the client's unconscious mind. While the Meta-Model encourages specificity and clarification, the Milton Model embraces ambiguity and flexibility to facilitate deep trance states and enhance hypnotic communication. Understanding the nuances of these two models is crucial for practitioners to effectively navigate various communication contexts within NLP.

IX. CALIBRATION TECHNIQUES

Calibration techniques play a crucial role in NLP by helping individuals develop a heightened sense of awareness and sensitivity to the verbal and non-verbal cues of others. By accurately "calibrating" to someone's physiology, tone of voice, and body language, practitioners of NLP can establish rapport more effectively and tailor their communication to better suit the needs of the other person. This skill is particularly useful in resolving conflicts, building trust, and fostering understanding in various social contexts. Through the use of calibration techniques, individuals can fine-tune their communication style to match the preferences and communication patterns of others, leading to more meaningful and impactful interactions. By emphasizing the importance of calibration, NLP empowers individuals to become more perceptive communicators and enhance their ability to connect with others on a deeper level.

Definition and importance of calibration

Calibration, a fundamental concept in NLP , plays a crucial role in effective communication. Defined as the ability to read and interpret subtle cues in others such as changes in tone of voice, body language, and facial expressions, calibration enables individuals to better understand the emotions, intentions, and attitudes of those they interact with. By honing this skill, one can establish rapport, build trust, and enhance overall communication effectiveness. In the context of NLP techniques, calibration serves as a powerful tool for matching and mirroring the behaviors of others, resulting in improved connection and influence.

Without calibration, communication can easily be misinterpreted or misunderstood, leading to conflicts or barriers in relationships. Therefore, mastering the art of calibration is essential for anyone seeking to navigate the complexities of human interaction and achieve successful communication outcomes.

Reading and interpreting non-verbal cues

One of the key aspects of effective communication that is emphasized in NLP is the ability to read and interpret non-verbal cues. Non-verbal communication plays a crucial role in conveying emotions, intentions, and attitudes, often more so than verbal language alone. By paying attention to body language, facial expressions, tone of voice, and other non-verbal signals, individuals can gain a deeper understanding of the underlying messages being communicated. Through the practice of calibration, individuals can fine-tune their sensitivity to these cues, allowing them to adjust their own communication style accordingly. Furthermore, mastering the skill of interpreting non-verbal cues enables individuals to establish rapport more effectively, build trust, and facilitate smoother interactions. Ultimately, incorporating the assessment and utilization of non-verbal cues into communication strategies can lead to more nuanced and successful interpersonal exchanges.

Calibration exercises for enhanced communication

The process of calibration plays an essential role in enhancing communication effectiveness within the realm of NLP . Through calibration exercises, individuals can develop a heightened sensitivity to verbal and non-verbal cues, allowing them to better understand the thoughts, emotions, and intentions of others. By fine-tuning their ability to observe micro-expressions, subtle changes in tone of voice, and body language cues, practitioners of NLP can adjust their own communication style to establish deeper rapport and connection with their interlocutors. This level of attunement enables individuals to adapt their messaging to be more resonant, persuasive, and impactful, leading to more successful interactions and outcomes. Ultimately, calibration exercises serve as a foundational tool in the NLP toolkit, empowering individuals to navigate complex social dynamics with greater ease and effectiveness.

X. ANCHORING TECHNIQUES

Anchoring techniques in NLP play a crucial role in shaping communication strategies. By creating associations between specific stimuli and desired emotional states, individuals can effectively influence their own and others' responses in various situations. Anchoring involves the intentional pairing of a particular sensory experience with a specific emotional or mental state, enabling individuals to access and maintain desired feelings or behaviors when needed. Through the use of anchors, individuals can trigger past positive experiences in order to enhance confidence, motivation, or resilience in challenging circumstances. Moreover, anchors can be strategically used to shift unproductive patterns of thinking or behavior towards more constructive outcomes. The power of anchoring lies in its ability to tap into the subconscious mind and leverage the connection between stimuli and emotional responses, ultimately leading to enhanced communication effectiveness and personal growth.

Concept of anchoring in NLP

One significant concept within NLP is the idea of anchoring, a powerful tool that can be utilized to manage emotions and influence behavior. Anchoring involves associating a specific trigger—such as a touch, gesture, or word—with a particular emotional state or response. By consciously creating and anchoring positive emotional states, individuals can access these resourceful states whenever needed, ultimately enhancing communication and decision-making processes. For instance, a leader could anchor confidence before a high-pressure presentation or an individual could anchor calmness before a difficult conversation. Understanding how anchoring works and how to effectively implement it can greatly impact one's ability to connect with others and achieve desired outcomes. By incorporating anchoring techniques into everyday interactions, individuals can become more attuned to their own emotions and better adept at influencing the emotions of others, leading to more successful communication and interpersonal relationships.

Types of anchors and their uses

Anchoring is a powerful NLP technique that involves associating a particular state of mind with a specific trigger or stimulus. There are various types of anchors that can be utilized in different situations to elicit desired responses. For example, a visual anchor could be a specific gesture or image that helps to bring about a particular feeling or emotion. Auditory anchors, on the other hand, involve using a specific sound or tone to evoke a certain state. Kinesthetic anchors target the sense of touch and can be a touch on the shoulder or a handshake that triggers a specific response. These anchors can be used to help individuals access resourceful states, overcome limiting beliefs, or shift unproductive behaviors. By strategically employing different types of anchors, individuals can enhance their communication skills, build rapport with others, and ultimately achieve their desired outcomes in various scenarios.

Establishing and utilizing anchors effectively

One fundamental aspect of NLP that contributes significantly to effective communication is the establishment and utilization of anchors. Anchors are stimuli that elicit specific emotional or physiological responses, creating powerful associations in the mind. By anchoring positive states like confidence, motivation, or relaxation to specific triggers, individuals can access these states at will during communication events, enhancing their presence and impact. Anchors can be physical, such as a touch or a gesture, or auditory, like a word or a tone, providing a versatile toolkit for establishing rapport and influencing outcomes. Understanding how to create, set, and fire anchors strategically allows communicators to navigate challenging interactions with finesse, boost their persuasive abilities, and foster deeper connections with others. By mastering the art of anchoring, individuals can shape their communication dynamics and elevate their effectiveness in various personal and professional contexts, ultimately leading to greater success and fulfillment.

XI. REFRAMING IN COMMUNICATION

NLP's power lies in its ability to reframe communication, allowing individuals to shift perspectives and find new meaning in interactions. By reframing, communicators can transform limiting beliefs or negative situations into opportunities for growth and understanding. This technique not only enhances clarity in communication but also fosters empathy and connection with others. Through the process of reframing, individuals can break free from habitual thinking patterns and open themselves up to new possibilities and solutions. In professional settings, reframing can help leaders inspire teams and navigate challenging situations with resilience and creativity. In personal relationships, reframing can deepen understanding and foster trust by enabling individuals to see situations from multiple angles. Ultimately, mastering the art of reframing in communication empowers individuals to cultivate more meaningful and impactful relationships in all areas of life.

Definition and types of reframing

In the realm of NLP, reframing is a powerful tool that involves changing the perspective or context of a situation to alter its meaning and impact. This technique is a cornerstone of effective communication as it allows individuals to shift their perception and outlook, leading to new insights and possibilities. There are several types of reframing that can be used in different contexts. Cognitive reframing involves changing the way one thinks about a situation to create a more positive or empowering interpretation. Emotional reframing focuses on altering the emotional response to a particular event by changing the emotional meaning attached to it. Behavioral reframing involves changing actions or behaviors associated with a situation to achieve a different outcome. By understanding and utilizing these various types of reframing, individuals can enhance their communication skills, resolve conflicts, and foster better relationships both personally and professionally.

Techniques for cognitive and context reframing

As individuals strive to enhance their communication skills through NLP , techniques for cognitive and context reframing emerge as powerful tools for transforming perspectives and fostering better understanding. By engaging in cognitive reframing, individuals can challenge and change limiting beliefs or negative thought patterns that may hinder effective communication. This process involves consciously shifting one's mindset to create new interpretations of situations and allowing for more positive outcomes. Context reframing, on the other hand, involves viewing a situation from different angles or contexts to gain a deeper understanding of the underlying dynamics at play. By leveraging these techniques, individuals can navigate complex communication scenarios with increased clarity and empathy, leading to more meaningful connections and productive interactions. Through practice and application, cognitive and context reframing can empower individuals to communicate authentically, build stronger relationships, and achieve their communication goals with greater confidence and effectiveness.

Impact of reframing on interpersonal interactions

The impact of reframing on interpersonal interactions is a crucial aspect of NLP that can significantly enhance communication dynamics. By reframing a situation or problem, individuals can shift their perspective and see things from a different angle, leading to more effective and positive interactions. This technique allows individuals to break free from limiting beliefs or negative patterns, opening up new possibilities for understanding and connection. In interpersonal relationships, reframing can help resolve conflicts, foster empathy, and promote mutual respect. By practicing reframing, individuals can navigate challenging conversations with more ease and grace, ultimately improving the quality of their relationships. Through the lens of NLP, reframing becomes a powerful tool for transforming communication barriers into opportunities for growth and connection.

XII. STRATEGIES FOR CONFLICT RESOLUTION

In the exploration of NLP , strategies for conflict resolution play a crucial role in enhancing effective communication. NLP offers a variety of tools that can be applied to navigate and resolve conflicts in both personal and professional settings. By utilizing techniques such as reframing, individuals can reframe the way they perceive conflicts, leading to more constructive outcomes. Additionally, the concept of calibration enables individuals to better understand the underlying motivations and emotions of others involved in the conflict, allowing for a more empathetic and nuanced approach to resolution. NLP techniques also emphasize building rapport and trust, which are essential for fostering open communication and finding common ground during conflicts. By learning and implementing these strategies for conflict resolution, individuals can not only improve their communication skills but also cultivate healthier and more productive relationships in all areas of their lives.

NLP approaches to managing conflicts

In the realm of conflict management, NLP approaches offer valuable tools for navigating difficult situations with empathy and understanding. By leveraging techniques like mirroring and pacing, individuals can establish rapport and create a sense of connection that paves the way for constructive dialogue. Through the process of reframing, conflicting parties can shift their perspectives and find common ground, leading to more mutually beneficial outcomes. Additionally, the use of language patterns and sensory acuity can help individuals better interpret the underlying emotions and motivations driving the conflict, enabling them to respond with greater sensitivity and insight. By incorporating NLP strategies into conflict resolution efforts, individuals can cultivate a more harmonious and productive environment where differences are embraced as opportunities for growth and understanding. These approaches not only empower individuals to manage conflicts more effectively but also foster deeper connections and strengthen relationships in the process.

Role of language patterns in conflict resolution

Language patterns play a crucial role in conflict resolution, as they can either escalate or de-escalate tense situations. By understanding the nuances of communication, individuals can navigate conflicts more effectively and reach mutually beneficial outcomes. Through NLP , practitioners can learn to identify and modify language patterns that may contribute to misunderstandings or escalate emotions. Techniques such as mirroring, pacing, and leading can be used to establish rapport and foster empathy, creating a conducive environment for resolving conflicts. Additionally, reframing negative language patterns into more positive and constructive ones can shift perspectives and open up new possibilities for resolution. Ultimately, mastering language patterns in conflict resolution allows individuals to communicate more effectively, build trust, and find common ground even in the most challenging situations.

Case studies on successful conflict resolution using NLP

One compelling case study in the realm of successful conflict resolution using NLP involves a team of sales professionals facing a significant interpersonal conflict. By applying NLP techniques such as mirroring and matching, the team leader was able to build rapport and establish a sense of trust among team members. Through effective communication and the use of language patterns, the leader facilitated open dialogue and encouraged a collaborative approach to resolving differences. Additionally, by employing anchoring techniques to evoke positive emotions and reframe negative perceptions, the team successfully navigated through conflicting viewpoints and reached a mutually beneficial solution. This case study exemplifies how NLP can be a powerful tool in mediating conflicts and fostering harmonious relationships within professional settings, ultimately leading to enhanced team dynamics and improved productivity.

XIII. NLP IN LEADERSHIP COMMUNICATION

NLP offers valuable tools that can transform leadership communication for the better. By delving into concepts such as calibration, anchoring, and reframing, individuals can develop a deeper understanding of how to connect with others effectively. Through case studies and practical examples, it becomes evident how these techniques can be applied in real-world scenarios to improve rapport and influence. Leaders who embrace NLP principles can enhance their ability to navigate complex interpersonal dynamics, communicate with clarity, and inspire others towards a common goal. The application of NLP in leadership communication not only fosters better understanding but also paves the way for more impactful interactions that yield positive outcomes. By incorporating NLP strategies into their communication repertoire, leaders can create a more conducive and engaging environment where their message resonates with others on a deeper level.

Enhancing leadership skills through NLP

NLP offers a valuable tool for individuals looking to enhance their leadership skills through improved communication techniques. By understanding how NLP principles can be applied in various situations, leaders can develop a deeper insight into verbal and non-verbal cues, allowing them to build stronger connections with their teams. Techniques such as calibration can help leaders better understand their team members' emotions and motivations, leading to more effective decision-making and conflict resolution. Anchoring techniques can be utilized to create positive associations with certain behaviors or outcomes, empowering leaders to inspire and motivate their teams. Additionally, reframing techniques can help leaders shift perspectives and find more effective solutions to challenges. By incorporating NLP strategies into their leadership approach, individuals can enhance their ability to influence, motivate, and lead others towards success.

NLP techniques for effective team management

In the realm of effective team management, NLP techniques offer a valuable toolkit for enhancing communication dynamics within a group setting. By leveraging NLP principles such as rapport-building, mirroring, and active listening, team leaders can establish strong connections with team members and foster a collaborative environment. Through the practice of calibration, leaders can attune themselves to the non-verbal cues and body language of team members to better understand their perspectives and emotions. Anchoring techniques can be employed to associate positive feelings with specific tasks or team achievements, motivating team members to excel in their responsibilities. Furthermore, the ability to reframe challenges as opportunities for growth and learning can help teams navigate conflicts and setbacks with resilience and a solutions-oriented mindset. Overall, integrating NLP techniques into team management practices can lead to improved communication, cohesion, and productivity within the team dynamic.

Case examples of NLP in leadership

In exploring case examples of NLP in leadership, it becomes evident how these techniques can be transformative in empowering individuals to become more effective and influential communicators. Leaders who have successfully applied NLP principles have been able to establish stronger connections with their teams, inspire trust and motivation, and navigate complex interpersonal dynamics with clarity and empathy. For instance, a study showcasing a CEO utilizing anchoring techniques to instill confidence in their team before a crucial presentation demonstrates the power of NLP in fostering a supportive and high-functioning work environment. By implementing reframing strategies, leaders can shift perspectives and resolve conflicts more constructively, leading to more harmonious relationships and increased productivity. These case studies underscore the practical applicability of NLP tools in real-world leadership contexts, highlighting their potential to enhance communication, drive success, and foster positive organizational culture.

XIV. NLP IN SALES AND MARKETING

In the realm of sales and marketing, NLP offers a powerful toolkit for professionals seeking to enhance their communication strategies. By understanding the intricacies of language patterns, behavioral cues, and the influence of emotions on decision-making, practitioners of NLP can tailor their approach to better resonate with potential clients and customers. Techniques such as mirroring and matching can help build rapport and establish trust, while reframing allows for the presentation of products or services in a more compelling light. The ability to calibrate and anchor specific responses can also aid in persuading individuals to take desired actions. Ultimately, integrating NLP into sales and marketing practices can lead to more effective communication, increased sales conversions, and stronger relationships with clients. By tapping into the principles of NLP, professionals can elevate their strategies and achieve greater success in the competitive market landscape.

Application of NLP in persuasive communication

The application of NLP in persuasive communication involves leveraging key techniques to influence and persuade others effectively. By utilizing techniques such as calibration, anchoring, and reframing, individuals can craft compelling messages that resonate with their audience and evoke desired responses. Through NLP, communicators can better understand the underlying motivations and beliefs of their audience, enabling them to tailor their messages for maximum impact. By honing their skills in NLP, individuals can build rapport, establish credibility, and ultimately persuade others to align with their viewpoints or take desired actions. Case studies and practical examples showcase how NLP can be a powerful tool in overcoming communication barriers and achieving persuasive outcomes in various situations. By incorporating NLP techniques into their communication strategies, individuals can enhance their ability to influence others positively and achieve their communication goals effectively.

Techniques for building customer rapport

As individuals seek to enhance their communication skills and build better connections with others, mastering techniques for building customer rapport becomes paramount. One effective method is through mirroring and matching, where one subtly mimics the body language, voice tone, and pacing of their customer to establish a sense of familiarity and trust. This technique can help create a harmonious interaction and facilitate smoother communication. Additionally, active listening plays a crucial role in building rapport by demonstrating genuine interest in the customer's perspectives and concerns. By engaging in attentive listening and asking relevant follow-up questions, one can show empathy and understanding, paving the way for a deeper connection. Ultimately, by incorporating these techniques into their communication repertoire, individuals can foster strong customer relationships, leading to increased loyalty, satisfaction, and ultimately, business success.

Case studies of NLP in sales success

In examining the application of NLP in sales success, various case studies highlight the effectiveness of NLP techniques in enhancing communication and influencing outcomes. These case studies provide valuable insights into how individuals can leverage NLP tools such as mirroring, pacing, and leading to establish rapport with clients, understand their needs, and guide them towards a purchasing decision. By analyzing real-world examples of successful sales interactions, researchers can identify patterns and strategies that contribute to closing deals and building long-lasting relationships with customers. These studies demonstrate the power of NLP in improving sales performance, boosting confidence, and creating a positive impact on the bottom line. Overall, the integration of NLP principles in sales settings offers a unique approach to communication that can drive success and achieve desired outcomes in a competitive marketplace.

XV. NLP IN EDUCATIONAL SETTINGS

In educational settings, NLP offers a unique approach to enhancing communication between educators and students. By understanding the power of language patterns, sensory systems, and beliefs, educators can tailor their teaching methods to cater to different learning styles and engage students more effectively. NLP techniques such as modeling successful behaviors, setting clear goals, and creating motivational anchors can empower students to overcome learning challenges and achieve their academic potential. Moreover, educators can use NLP to cultivate a positive learning environment, improve classroom management, and foster strong relationships with students based on trust and rapport. By integrating NLP into educational settings, teachers can not only enhance their own communication skills but also empower students to become more self-aware, confident, and successful learners. Through the application of NLP principles, educators can create a transformative learning experience that promotes growth, development, and academic excellence.

Role of NLP in teaching and learning

By incorporating NLP into teaching and learning practices, educators can profoundly impact the way students absorb information and engage with the material. NLP techniques can help teachers better understand their students' learning styles, preferences, and motivations, allowing them to tailor their approach to meet individual needs. Through effective communication strategies such as pacing and leading, teachers can establish rapport with students, creating a conducive learning environment. Additionally, NLP tools like anchoring can be used to enhance memory retention and boost student motivation. By incorporating NLP principles into lesson planning and classroom management, educators can foster a more dynamic and engaging learning experience for students. Ultimately, by leveraging the principles of NLP in teaching, educators can empower students to reach their full potential and achieve academic success.

NLP techniques for effective teaching

NLP techniques offer a wealth of possibilities for enhancing teaching effectiveness. By incorporating NLP principles into educational practices, educators can create a more engaging and impactful learning environment for their students. Techniques such as mirroring and matching can help teachers establish rapport with their students, fostering a more positive and productive classroom atmosphere. Additionally, anchoring techniques can be employed to associate positive emotions with learning tasks, increasing motivation and retention. Reframing techniques can also be valuable in addressing student challenges and promoting a growth mindset. By integrating these NLP techniques into their teaching approach, educators can not only improve student engagement and comprehension but also cultivate a more supportive and empowering learning experience. Overall, NLP techniques have the potential to revolutionize the field of education by empowering teachers to connect more effectively with their students and facilitate deeper learning and growth.

Impact of NLP on student engagement and learning outcomes

NLP has been found to have a significant impact on student engagement and learning outcomes in educational settings. By utilizing NLP techniques such as modeling, reframing, and rapport building, educators can create a more interactive and dynamic learning environment. Through effective communication strategies, teachers can better connect with students, tailor instruction to their individual needs, and ultimately enhance their overall learning experience. Research has shown that when students feel engaged and connected to their teachers, they are more likely to participate actively in class, retain information better, and achieve higher academic success. In this way, NLP not only improves communication between teachers and students but also has a tangible impact on learning outcomes. By integrating NLP practices into educational settings, educators can foster a more engaging and effective learning environment that promotes student success and holistic development.

XVI. NLP IN THERAPEUTIC CONTEXTS

Examining the application of NLP in therapeutic contexts reveals a transformative potential for enhancing communication and fostering personal growth. Therapists utilizing NLP techniques can effectively guide clients in understanding their thought patterns, emotional responses, and behavioral triggers, leading to increased self-awareness and empowerment. By incorporating NLP strategies such as reframing negative beliefs, establishing rapport through mirroring techniques, and utilizing language patterns to induce positive change, therapists can assist clients in overcoming mental health challenges and achieving desired outcomes. Case studies highlighting the successful integration of NLP in therapy underscore its effectiveness in promoting emotional healing, facilitating behavior modification, and improving overall well-being. In the therapeutic setting, NLP serves as a powerful tool for promoting resilience, self-discovery, and holistic growth, ultimately fostering a deeper connection between clients and their inner selves.

Use of NLP in counseling and therapy

In the realm of counseling and therapy, the integration of NLP has shown immense promise in enhancing the effectiveness of communication between therapists and clients. By incorporating NLP techniques such as mirroring, pacing, and leading, counselors can establish better rapport with their clients, ultimately fostering a more trusting and conducive environment for therapy. Moreover, NLP enables therapists to better understand the underlying beliefs and thought patterns of their clients through linguistic cues, allowing for deeper insights and tailored interventions. Through the application of NLP in counseling sessions, therapists can empower individuals to overcome limiting beliefs, reframe negative thought patterns, and achieve personal growth. Overall, the utilization of NLP in counseling and therapy exemplifies a powerful toolset that can significantly enhance the therapeutic process and promote positive outcomes for clients seeking mental health support.

Techniques for therapeutic communication

One of the key techniques for effective therapeutic communication within the realm of NLP is calibration. This process involves carefully observing and interpreting verbal and non-verbal cues to better understand a person's emotional state and intentions. By practicing active listening and paying attention to micro-expressions, tone of voice, and body language, individuals can develop a greater sense of empathy and build stronger rapport with others. In addition to calibration, anchoring is another powerful tool that can be utilized in therapeutic communication. This technique involves linking a specific stimulus with a desired emotional state, allowing individuals to access positive emotions or resources in times of need. By utilizing these techniques in a therapeutic setting, practitioners can create a safe and supportive environment for clients to express themselves and work towards positive growth and change.

Case studies of therapeutic outcomes using NLP

The efficacy of NLP in therapeutic settings is well-documented through various case studies showcasing positive outcomes.

These studies highlight the transformative power of NLP techniques in helping individuals overcome deep-seated issues, such as phobias, anxiety, and trauma. By utilizing tools like pattern interrupts, timeline therapy, and the Meta Model, therapists have been able to facilitate profound changes in clients' thoughts, emotions, and behaviors. Through a combination of linguistic patterns, cognitive strategies, and sensory-based interventions, NLP offers a comprehensive approach to address psychological issues and promote personal growth. Case studies demonstrate how NLP can empower individuals to reframe negative beliefs, release past traumas, and cultivate a more positive self-image. Overall, the evidence from these therapeutic outcomes underscores the value of NLP as a powerful and versatile tool for facilitating positive change and enhancing well-being.

XVII. NLP AND PERSONAL RELATIONSHIPS

The application of NLP in personal relationships can be profound, offering individuals a framework to enhance their communication skills and foster deeper connections. By understanding the key techniques of NLP such as calibration, anchoring, and reframing, individuals can improve their ability to interpret and respond to various cues in interpersonal interactions. Through the use of case studies and practical examples, the book illustrates how NLP can be utilized to navigate challenging situations, effectively resolve conflicts, and build trust in relationships. Furthermore, the incorporation of NLP techniques encourages individuals to reflect on their own communication styles, promoting self-awareness and mindfulness in their interactions. Ultimately, by harnessing the principles of NLP, individuals can cultivate more meaningful and harmonious relationships, fostering empathy, understanding, and mutual respect in their personal connections.

Improving personal interactions through NLP

By integrating NLP principles into personal interactions, individuals can enhance their communication skills and strengthen relationships. NLP techniques offer a systematic approach to understanding verbal and non-verbal cues, allowing individuals to better interpret and respond to others' messages. Techniques such as calibration, anchoring, and reframing provide tools for building rapport and influencing others positively. Through case studies and practical examples, it becomes evident how these techniques can break down communication barriers and facilitate goal achievement in various contexts. By incorporating NLP into their communication toolkit, individuals can not only improve their ability to express themselves clearly but also cultivate a better understanding of others' perspectives. Ultimately, NLP encourages individuals to adopt a more mindful and effective approach to communication, leading to more meaningful and fulfilling interactions in both personal and professional realms.

NLP strategies for deeper emotional connections

In the realm of NLP , strategies exist that can deepen emotional connections between individuals, paving the way for more profound and meaningful interactions. By harnessing techniques such as mirroring, pacing, and leading, practitioners of NLP can establish a strong rapport with others, fostering a sense of trust and understanding that transcends mere words. These strategies allow for a deeper level of empathy and emotional resonance, enabling communicators to truly connect on a heart-to-heart level. Through the use of NLP techniques, individuals can navigate complex emotional landscapes more effectively, leading to more authentic and fulfilling relationships. Ultimately, by incorporating these strategies into their communication repertoire, individuals can cultivate deeper emotional connections that lay the foundation for genuine and lasting bonds with others.

Examples of NLP improving personal life

In the realm of personal development, NLP has shown significant improvements in individuals' lives by enhancing self-awareness, emotional intelligence, and overall well-being. By utilizing NLP techniques such as visualization, reframing negative thoughts, and setting clear goals, individuals can overcome limiting beliefs, manage stress, and boost their self-confidence. For example, practicing NLP exercises can help individuals break free from destructive patterns of behavior, such as procrastination or self-sabotage, leading to improved productivity and a greater sense of fulfillment. Moreover, NLP aids in enhancing interpersonal relationships by fostering empathy, active listening, and effective communication skills. Through the application of NLP principles, individuals can cultivate stronger connections with others, resolve conflicts peacefully, and create a harmonious environment in both personal and professional spheres. Ultimately, the practice of NLP offers a holistic approach to personal growth and empowers individuals to lead more fulfilling and meaningful lives.

XVIII. NLP FOR PUBLIC SPEAKING

NLP offers a wealth of tools and techniques that can significantly enhance an individual's public speaking skills. By honing the ability to read verbal and non-verbal cues, speakers can calibrate their message for maximum impact, engaging their audience on a deeper level. Anchoring techniques can help control emotions and anchor positive associations to specific speaking situations, thereby boosting confidence and charisma on stage. Moreover, the power of reframing allows speakers to shift perspective and present their ideas in a more compelling and persuasive manner. Through case studies and practical examples, it is evident that mastering NLP concepts can transform public speaking from a daunting task to a confident and influential performance. By incorporating NLP strategies into their communication arsenal, individuals can deliver more effective speeches, connect with their audience on a profound level, and leave a lasting impact.

Techniques to enhance public speaking skills

By utilizing NLP techniques, individuals can develop and enhance their public speaking skills. Techniques such as visualization, mirroring, and pacing help speakers connect with their audience on a deeper level, building rapport and trust. Visualization techniques can aid in reducing anxiety and boosting confidence, allowing speakers to deliver their message with clarity and impact. Mirroring, where the speaker subtly mirrors the body language and speech patterns of their audience, helps establish a sense of familiarity and understanding. Pacing, the act of matching the tempo and tone of the audience, creates a harmonious flow of communication. These techniques not only improve the speaker's ability to engage and persuade their audience but also enhance their overall presence and authority. Through the application of NLP principles, individuals can master the art of public speaking and effectively convey their message to diverse audiences.

Role of NLP in audience engagement

In exploring the role of NLP in audience engagement, it becomes evident that NLP techniques play a crucial part in enhancing communication effectiveness. By understanding the intricacies of NLP, individuals can grasp the nuances of verbal and non-verbal cues, allowing them to build rapport and connect with their audience on a deeper level. Techniques such as calibration, anchoring, and reframing are fundamental in not only decoding the audience's responses but also in shaping the interaction towards a more positive outcome. Through the application of NLP concepts, communicators can navigate through barriers, adapt their approach, and influence their audience in meaningful ways. By incorporating NLP principles into their communication strategies, individuals can foster engagement, establish trust, and ultimately, achieve their desired outcomes when interacting with different audiences.

Examples of successful public speakers using NLP

Public speakers who have successfully utilized NLP techniques serve as exemplary role models for those looking to enhance their communication skills. One notable example is Tony Robbins, a renowned motivational speaker known for his ability to captivate and inspire audiences using NLP strategies. By incorporating language patterns, sensory acuity, and rapport-building techniques, Robbins has been able to establish a strong connection with his listeners and effectively convey his messages. Similarly, former US President Barack Obama has been praised for his charismatic and persuasive speaking style, which is believed to be influenced by NLP principles. Obama's use of metaphors, pacing and leading, and well-timed pauses have all contributed to his success as a public speaker. These examples demonstrate the real-world application of NLP in enhancing communication effectiveness and influencing positive change in both professional and personal contexts.

XIX. NLP AND NON-VERBAL COMMUNICATION

NLP, as a powerful tool for enhancing communication, also delves into the realm of non-verbal communication. Understanding non-verbal cues is crucial in decoding the true intentions and emotions of others. By studying body language, facial expressions, and tone of voice, individuals can gain deeper insights into the messages being conveyed. NLP techniques such as mirroring and matching can be utilized to build rapport and establish connections on a subconscious level, fostering trust and understanding. Moreover, NLP helps individuals become more aware of their own non-verbal signals, allowing them to align their words with their body language for a more coherent and authentic communication style. By incorporating non-verbal communication into the NLP framework, individuals can become more adept at deciphering hidden meanings and creating meaningful connections in various contexts, ultimately leading to more effective and harmonious interactions.

Understanding body language through NLP

In the realm of NLP , understanding body language holds a crucial place in enhancing communication effectiveness. By deciphering the non-verbal cues that individuals emit, one can gain a deeper insight into their thoughts, feelings, and intentions. Through NLP techniques such as calibration, practitioners can fine-tune their ability to interpret subtle gestures, facial expressions, and posture, thereby increasing their capacity to build rapport and establish connections with others. Anchoring, another key concept in NLP, allows individuals to link specific emotions or states to particular gestures or stimuli, enabling them to evoke desired responses in themselves and others. Moreover, reframing techniques in NLP offer a powerful tool for reshaping perspectives and shifting communication dynamics. By delving into the nuances of body language through the lens of NLP, individuals can navigate interpersonal interactions with more sensitivity, insight, and effectiveness.

Techniques to interpret and use body language effectively

An important aspect of utilizing NLP techniques is the ability to interpret and use body language effectively. By understanding non-verbal cues such as facial expressions, gestures, and posture, individuals can gain valuable insights into the thoughts and feelings of others, leading to more meaningful interactions. Through techniques such as mirroring and matching, individuals can establish rapport and build connections with others on a subconscious level. Additionally, being able to read and interpret microexpressions can provide deeper insight into a person's true emotions, allowing for more accurate communication and enhanced empathy. By incorporating these body language techniques into everyday interactions, individuals can become more persuasive communicators, better equipped to navigate a variety of social situations with confidence and success. In essence, mastering the interpretation and utilization of body language is a key component of effective communication and can significantly impact the quality of relationships and interactions in both personal and professional settings.

The impact of non-verbal cues in communication

The impact of non-verbal cues in communication cannot be overstated when it comes to the effectiveness of interpersonal interactions. Research has shown that a significant portion of communication is conveyed through non-verbal cues such as body language, facial expressions, and tone of voice. These cues can often convey more meaning and emotion than words alone, making them a crucial aspect of understanding the true message being communicated. In the context of NLP , the ability to decode and interpret these non-verbal cues plays a key role in building rapport, establishing trust, and influencing others positively. By honing skills in reading and responding to non-verbal cues, individuals can enhance their communication abilities and better connect with others on a deeper level. This heightened awareness of non-verbal communication can ultimately lead to more effective and impactful interactions in both personal and professional settings.

XX. NLP AND DIGITAL COMMUNICATION

In the realm of NLP and digital communication, the fusion of technology and NLP techniques opens up new possibilities for enhancing interpersonal interactions in the digital age. With the rise of social media, messaging platforms, and virtual meetings, the need for effective communication strategies has never been more crucial. By integrating NLP principles into digital communication practices, individuals can improve their ability to convey ideas clearly, build rapport, and influence others positively through virtual channels. Techniques such as mirroring, pacing, and leading can be adapted to online environments to establish trust and understanding. Moreover, the use of visual aids, emoticons, and multimedia content can complement NLP strategies to enhance engagement and convey emotions effectively. In this digital landscape, mastering NLP techniques is not just beneficial but essential for navigating the complexities of modern communication platforms and fostering meaningful connections in a virtual world.

Adapting NLP techniques for digital platforms

In the digital age, the field of NLP is increasingly being adapted to suit the demands of online platforms. With the rise of virtual communication, there is a growing need to optimize NLP techniques for digital interactions. By harnessing the power of technology, practitioners can now leverage tools such as video conferencing, chatbots, and social media platforms to enhance communication effectiveness. Virtual reality simulations and AI algorithms can be used to create immersive experiences that facilitate rapport-building and empathy development, crucial components of NLP. Moreover, the integration of data analytics and machine learning can provide insights into communication patterns and suggest personalized strategies for individuals to improve their interactions online. As digital platforms continue to evolve, the adaptation of NLP techniques to suit these environments will be essential in ensuring effective communication and relationship-building in the virtual realm.

Challenges and solutions for virtual communication

In the realm of virtual communication, numerous challenges can hinder effective interaction. The absence of non-verbal cues such as facial expressions and body language can lead to misunderstandings and misinterpretations. Technical issues like poor internet connectivity or audio problems can disrupt the flow of conversations and decrease engagement. Moreover, the lack of immediate feedback in virtual settings can make it difficult to gauge the effectiveness of one's communication and make necessary adjustments in real-time. However, innovative solutions can address these challenges and enhance virtual communication. Utilizing video conferencing platforms that offer features like screen sharing and virtual backgrounds can make interactions more dynamic and engaging. Establishing clear communication norms and setting expectations for virtual meetings can help ensure all participants are on the same page. Implementing regular check-ins, feedback sessions, and virtual team-building activities can foster a sense of connection and collaboration among remote team members. By recognizing and adapting to the unique challenges of virtual communication, individuals can cultivate more effective and meaningful interactions in a digital environment.

Case studies of effective digital communication using NLP

In the realm of digital communication, case studies have showcased the effectiveness of integrating NLP techniques. By leveraging NLP principles such as mirroring, pacing, and leading, organizations have been able to create more engaging and authentic interactions with their target audiences. For instance, a study conducted on a social media marketing campaign revealed that incorporating NLP techniques in the copywriting and content creation process resulted in higher levels of audience engagement and conversion rates. Another case study focused on customer service interactions showed that using NLP strategies to enhance empathy and active listening skills led to a significant improvement in customer satisfaction and loyalty. These examples highlight the power of NLP in fostering meaningful connections and driving successful digital communication strategies. By analyzing these cases, professionals can gain valuable insights into how to apply NLP effectively in their own digital communication efforts to achieve desired outcomes.

XXI. ETHICAL CONSIDERATIONS IN NLP

As individuals delve into the realm of NLP , it becomes imperative to address the ethical considerations that underpin its practice. Ethical dilemmas in NLP can arise when practitioners utilize techniques to manipulate or deceive others for personal gain, rather than fostering genuine understanding and connection. By acknowledging the power dynamics inherent in communication, NLP practitioners must uphold ethical standards that prioritize respect, honesty, and consent. A crucial aspect of ethical NLP practice involves ensuring that individuals are aware of the techniques being used and that they are implemented in a transparent and empowering manner. Additionally, practitioners must consider the potential impact of their actions on individuals' mental and emotional well-being, avoiding manipulative tactics that could harm trust and relationships. Ultimately, ethical considerations in NLP serve as a guiding compass, directing practitioners towards authenticity, empathy, and ethical communication practices.

Ethical issues surrounding the use of NLP

One of the key ethical considerations surrounding the use of NLP is the potential for manipulation or coercion in communication. NLP techniques, such as anchoring and reframing, can be powerful tools for influencing others' thoughts and behaviors. However, when used unethically, these strategies have the potential to deceive or manipulate individuals for personal gain. It is crucial for practitioners of NLP to be aware of the ethical implications of their use of these techniques and to prioritize honesty, transparency, and respect for the autonomy of others. Additionally, the issue of consent is paramount in NLP practices, as individuals should have full knowledge and understanding of how their communication is being shaped or influenced. By upholding ethical standards and being mindful of the impact of their communication techniques, practitioners can ensure that NLP is used responsibly and ethically to enhance relationships and promote positive outcomes.

Guidelines for ethical practice in NLP

As individuals delve into the intricate realm of NLP , it becomes paramount to adhere to guidelines for ethical practice to ensure its efficacy and impact. Ethical considerations in NLP encompass respecting the autonomy and well-being of individuals involved, maintaining confidentiality, and obtaining informed consent. Practitioners must strive for transparency and honesty in their communication, avoiding manipulation or coercion. Furthermore, practitioners should continuously assess and enhance their skills through ongoing training and supervision to uphold professional standards and safeguard the interests of their clients. By integrating ethical principles into NLP practice, practitioners can cultivate trust, foster positive relationships, and facilitate meaningful change in individuals seeking personal growth and development. Ultimately, ethical guidelines in NLP not only serve to protect the integrity of the practice but also contribute to the well-being and empowerment of those engaged in the process.

The importance of integrity in NLP applications

In the realm of NLP , the significance of integrity cannot be overstated, particularly when it comes to its applications. Integrity in NLP refers to the practice of aligning one's words, actions, and intentions in a coherent manner, ensuring authenticity and honesty in communication. When practitioners uphold integrity in their interactions, they establish trust, credibility, and rapport with others, which are essential components for effective communication. Integrity serves as the foundation upon which NLP techniques can truly flourish, allowing individuals to navigate complex social dynamics with transparency and respect. By embodying integrity, NLP practitioners can ethically leverage tools such as calibration, anchoring, and reframing to influence others positively and foster harmonious relationships. Ultimately, the integration of integrity in NLP applications not only enhances communication effectiveness but also contributes to the ethical practice and responsible utilization of these powerful techniques.

XXII. MEASURING THE EFFECTIVENESS OF NLP

As the exploration of NLP progresses, the need to measure its effectiveness becomes paramount. Various methods can be employed to assess the impact of NLP techniques on communication outcomes. One approach involves utilizing pre- and post-assessments to gauge changes in communication skills, confidence levels, and interpersonal relationships before and after NLP interventions. Additionally, qualitative research methods such as interviews and focus groups can provide valuable insights into how individuals perceive the effectiveness of NLP in their specific contexts. Objective measures, such as observing non-verbal behaviors during interactions or analyzing the language patterns used before and after NLP training, can offer tangible data to evaluate the effectiveness of NLP techniques. By employing a multi-faceted assessment approach that combines quantitative and qualitative measures, researchers can gain a comprehensive understanding of how NLP impacts communication effectiveness across diverse settings.

Criteria for evaluating NLP outcomes

NLP outcomes can be evaluated based on various criteria that gauge the effectiveness and efficiency of the techniques used. One crucial aspect to consider is the level of rapport established between the communicator and the recipient. The ability to build trust and connection through NLP strategies such as mirroring and matching is indicative of successful outcomes. Additionally, the clarity and precision of communication is essential in assessing the impact of NLP interventions. The ability to convey messages in a concise and understandable manner can determine the effectiveness of the communication. Furthermore, the ability to influence and persuade through NLP techniques like reframing and anchoring can be valuable indicators of outcomes. Ultimately, the criteria for evaluating NLP outcomes should focus on the improvement in communication skills, the establishment of rapport, and the successful achievement of desired goals through effective use of NLP techniques.

Research methodologies for studying NLP

Research methodologies for studying NLP encompass a range of approaches aimed at understanding the mechanisms behind this complex framework of communication and behavior modification. Qualitative methods such as interviews, case studies, and content analysis can provide insight into the subjective experiences of individuals who have undergone NLP interventions, shedding light on the transformative effects of these techniques. In contrast, quantitative methods like surveys and experiments offer opportunities to measure the effectiveness of specific NLP interventions objectively, allowing researchers to gather empirical evidence to support the claims of NLP proponents. Mixed-method approaches, combining both qualitative and quantitative techniques, can provide a more comprehensive understanding of the phenomena under study, bridging the gap between subjective experiences and empirical data. By employing a diverse array of research methodologies, scholars can elucidate the underlying processes of NLP, contributing to its continued development and application in various contexts.

Analysis of empirical studies on NLP's effectiveness

Numerous empirical studies have been conducted to assess the effectiveness of NLP techniques in enhancing communication. These studies delve into various aspects of NLP, such as its impact on building rapport, improving persuasion skills, and increasing emotional intelligence. Through the analysis of these studies, it becomes evident that NLP can be a powerful tool in improving communication outcomes in a range of contexts. By understanding how NLP techniques such as mirroring, pacing, and leading can influence human behavior and perception, individuals can adapt their communication strategies to achieve better outcomes. The findings of these studies highlight the potential for NLP to enhance interpersonal relationships, leadership effectiveness, and overall communication success. Overall, the empirical evidence supports the value of NLP as a valuable tool for improving communication skills and achieving desired outcomes in various personal and professional settings.

XXIII. CRITICISMS AND CONTROVERSIES OF NLP

One of the main criticisms and controversies surrounding NLP revolves around the lack of empirical evidence to support its claims. Skeptics argue that NLP lacks a solid scientific foundation and that some of its techniques may be more placebo effects than actual effective tools for communication. Furthermore, the commercialization of NLP has drawn criticism as some practitioners make grandiose claims about its ability to bring about profound change without substantial evidence to back them up. Additionally, there have been concerns raised about the ethical implications of using NLP techniques to manipulate or influence others for personal gain. Despite these criticisms, proponents of NLP argue that the effectiveness of its principles lies in their practical application rather than in theoretical validation. They emphasize the importance of experiential learning and personal growth through NLP techniques in enhancing communication skills and fostering positive relationships.

Common criticisms of NLP practices

One common criticism of NLP practices revolves around the lack of scientific evidence to support its efficacy. Skeptics argue that the theoretical underpinnings of NLP are based on subjective experiences rather than empirical research, calling into question the validity of its claims. Additionally, some critics question the ethics of NLP techniques, particularly those related to persuasion and influence. They argue that the use of language patterns and manipulative strategies in NLP may be exploitative or deceptive in nature, leading to concerns about its potential misuse. Another critique of NLP practices is the oversimplification of complex psychological processes. Critics argue that NLP's models and techniques may provide a superficial understanding of human behavior, ignoring the intricacies and individual differences that shape communication dynamics. Despite these criticisms, proponents of NLP argue that when used responsibly and ethically, NLP can be a powerful tool for enhancing communication and personal development.

Responses to criticisms from the NLP community

Upon encountering criticisms from the NLP community, it is crucial to address them with a thoughtful and well-informed response. One common critique revolves around the perceived lack of scientific evidence supporting the effectiveness of NLP techniques. In response, researchers and practitioners must emphasize the empirical studies and real-world applications that attest to the benefits of NLP in enhancing communication and personal development. Additionally, it is important to acknowledge any valid concerns raised by critics and engage in constructive dialogue to foster a deeper understanding of NLP principles. By actively engaging with the criticisms from the NLP community, practitioners can refine their techniques, incorporate feedback, and evolve the field in a positive direction. Ultimately, responding to these criticisms with openness and a willingness to learn can lead to a more robust and respected discipline that continues to empower individuals in their communication endeavors.

The scientific validity of NLP

The scientific validity of NLP has been a subject of debate within the psychological community. Critics argue that the lack of empirical evidence and the reliance on anecdotal experiences diminish the credibility of NLP as a valid therapeutic approach. However, proponents of NLP assert that its foundation in cognitive psychology, linguistics, and neuroscience provides a solid theoretical framework for understanding human behavior and communication. Studies have shown that NLP techniques can be effective in improving self-awareness, enhancing communication skills, and facilitating personal growth. While more robust research is needed to establish NLP's effectiveness conclusively, the integration of NLP principles into various fields demonstrates its practical value in achieving desired outcomes. By combining insights from psychology and linguistics, NLP offers a unique perspective on how language and behavior influence one another, paving the way for more effective communication strategies.

XXIV. NLP TRAINING AND CERTIFICATION

NLP training and certification play a crucial role in equipping individuals with the necessary skills to effectively implement NLP techniques in various contexts. Through structured coursework and hands-on practice, participants can deepen their understanding of NLP principles and gain confidence in applying them in real-world scenarios. Certification provides a stamp of approval, indicating to employers, clients, or peers that an individual has met certain standards of proficiency in NLP. This not only enhances credibility but also opens up new opportunities for career advancement or consultancy roles where NLP expertise is sought after. Moreover, formal training programs often involve supervised practice sessions and feedback, allowing participants to hone their skills under the guidance of experienced trainers. In a rapidly evolving field like NLP, ongoing training and certification serve as a means to stay current with the latest developments and refine one's craft for optimal effectiveness.

Overview of NLP training programs

NLP training programs encompass a wide range of offerings tailored to various objectives and levels of expertise. From introductory courses providing a basic understanding of NLP principles to advanced programs focusing on specialized applications, individuals can choose the training program that best suits their needs. These programs typically combine theoretical knowledge with hands-on practical exercises to ensure comprehensive learning and skill development. Furthermore, reputable NLP training programs are often led by experienced practitioners and trainers who can provide valuable insights and guidance based on real-world experience. Participants in these programs can expect to enhance their communication skills, improve interpersonal relationships, and cultivate a deeper understanding of human behavior and cognition. Overall, NLP training programs offer a structured and systematic approach to mastering the techniques and strategies of NLP, empowering individuals to unlock their full communicative potential and achieve greater success in both personal and professional endeavors.

Criteria for choosing the right NLP course

When considering which NLP course to choose, several key criteria should be taken into account to ensure that the selected program meets the individual's needs and goals. First and foremost, it is essential to evaluate the credibility and reputation of the course provider. Look for institutions or trainers with a solid track record in the field of NLP, as well as relevant certifications and endorsements from reputable organizations. Additionally, the curriculum and content of the course should align with the specific areas of interest or expertise one wishes to develop. Whether it be communication skills, personal development, or therapeutic applications, the course should offer a comprehensive and well-rounded approach to NLP techniques. Lastly, practical considerations such as course duration, format (in-person or online), and cost should also be taken into consideration to ensure that the course fits comfortably into one's schedule and budget. By carefully assessing these factors, individuals can make an informed decision when selecting the right NLP course for their personal and professional development needs.

The significance of certification in NLP practice

A crucial aspect of practicing NLP lies in the significance of certification. Certification in NLP not only provides practitioners with a formal validation of their skills and knowledge but also demonstrates a commitment to ethical standards and professional development. By obtaining certification, individuals can differentiate themselves in the field, gaining credibility and trust from clients and colleagues. Furthermore, certification in NLP signifies a dedication to ongoing learning and growth, as practitioners must engage in continuing education to maintain their certification. This constant pursuit of knowledge and refinement of skills ensures that certified NLP practitioners are equipped to deliver high-quality services and adapt to the ever-evolving landscape of communication. In essence, certification in NLP serves as a mark of excellence, professionalism, and commitment to the practice, setting certified practitioners apart as experts in the field.

XXV. FUTURE DIRECTIONS IN NLP RESEARCH

As the field of NLP continues to evolve, future directions in research offer exciting possibilities for enhancing communication practices. One key area of focus is the exploration of advanced technologies, such as AI and machine learning, to develop more sophisticated NLP algorithms. These technologies could revolutionize how NLP tools are used in various contexts, from customer service chatbots to language translation systems. Additionally, there is a growing emphasis on interdisciplinary collaborations, with researchers from psychology, linguistics, and computer science working together to deepen our understanding of how language shapes our interactions. Future research may also delve into the impact of cultural differences on NLP effectiveness, leading to more nuanced and culturally sensitive communication techniques. By embracing cutting-edge technologies and fostering interdisciplinary collaboration, the future of NLP research holds great promise in unlocking new ways to enhance communication skills and achieve more meaningful connections.

Emerging trends in NLP

Within the realm of NLP , there are emerging trends that are shaping the way individuals approach communication. One notable trend is the emphasis on ethical considerations in NLP practices, urging practitioners to prioritize transparency, consent, and respect in all interactions. Another trend involves the integration of technology and AI into NLP techniques, allowing for more personalized and efficient communication strategies.

Additionally, there is a growing focus on cultural competency in NLP, recognizing the importance of understanding diverse cultural norms and values to facilitate effective communication across different contexts. These emerging trends highlight the evolving nature of NLP and the need for practitioners to adapt their approaches to meet the changing demands of communication in today's complex world. By incorporating these trends into NLP practices, individuals can enhance their communication skills and navigate interpersonal interactions with greater awareness and efficacy.

Potential new applications of NLP techniques

In addition to the traditional applications of NLP techniques in communication and personal development, there is a growing interest in exploring new potential uses for these tools. One such area is in the field of AI and machine learning, where NLP can be leveraged to improve the accuracy and efficiency of natural language processing tasks. By incorporating NLP algorithms into chatbots, virtual assistants, and other AI-driven systems, developers can enhance the conversational capabilities and understanding of these technologies. Furthermore, NLP techniques could also be applied in the healthcare sector to analyze patient data, identify patterns in symptoms, and improve diagnostic accuracy. As technology continues to advance, the integration of NLP methods in these emerging fields holds great promise for revolutionizing the way we communicate, interact, and make decisions in a wide range of domains.

The future of NLP in technology integration

As technology continues to advance at a rapid pace, the future of NLP in technology integration holds immense potential. With the rise of AI, machine learning, and natural language processing, NLP techniques can be leveraged to enhance human-computer interaction. By incorporating NLP principles into digital interfaces, software programs, and virtual assistants, developers can create more intuitive and user-friendly systems that effectively communicate with users in a more natural and personalized manner. Moreover, NLP in technology integration can enable real-time language translation, sentiment analysis, and personalized recommendations, revolutionizing the way we interact with machines. As we move towards a more interconnected and digitized world, the integration of NLP into technology will play a crucial role in optimizing user experience and driving innovation in various sectors, from healthcare to finance to education. The possibilities are endless as we unlock the full potential of NLP in shaping the future of technology integration.

XXVI. NLP AND EMOTIONAL INTELLIGENCE

Understanding emotional intelligence plays a crucial role in the realm of NLP . By fusing the principles of NLP with emotional intelligence, individuals can develop a deeper awareness of their own emotions and the emotions of others, leading to more effective communication. This integration empowers individuals to recognize and regulate their emotions, empathize with others, and navigate social interactions with greater skill and sensitivity. NLP techniques such as mirroring and pacing can be enhanced by emotional intelligence, allowing for a more authentic and empathetic connection with others. Ultimately, the synergy between NLP and emotional intelligence offers a comprehensive approach to communication that not only focuses on the words spoken but also the underlying emotional context. As individuals cultivate their emotional intelligence through NLP practices, they equip themselves with the tools necessary to foster positive relationships, resolve conflicts, and achieve greater personal and professional success.

Relationship between NLP and emotional intelligence

One intriguing aspect of NLP is its relationship with emotional intelligence, as both concepts share a common focus on understanding and managing human emotions. By incorporating NLP techniques, individuals can enhance their emotional intelligence by developing a deeper awareness of their own thoughts, feelings, and behaviors, as well as those of others. This heightened self-awareness allows individuals to communicate more effectively, build stronger relationships, and navigate challenging situations with greater ease. NLP provides tools for recognizing and regulating emotions, as well as strategies for empathizing with and influencing others. Through the integration of NLP and emotional intelligence, individuals can cultivate a well-rounded skill set that enables them to navigate complex interpersonal dynamics and achieve their communication goals with precision and emotional acuity. This symbiotic relationship between NLP and emotional intelligence underscores the profound impact these two frameworks can have on personal and professional success.

NLP techniques to enhance emotional awareness

As individuals strive to improve their communication skills, the utilization of NLP techniques presents a valuable opportunity to enhance emotional awareness. By delving into the intricacies of NLP, individuals can gain insight into not only their own emotional responses but also those of others, allowing for more empathetic and effective interactions. Through practices such as calibration, individuals can learn to accurately read and interpret subtle non-verbal cues, fostering a deeper understanding of emotions in both themselves and those they communicate with. Furthermore, techniques like anchoring can be employed to create positive emotional states and reinforce desired behaviors, leading to more harmonious relationships and successful outcomes. By integrating NLP techniques into their communication repertoire, individuals can cultivate emotional intelligence and elevate their ability to connect with others on a more profound level.

Case studies on emotional intelligence improvement through NLP

As demonstrated in various case studies, the application of NLP techniques has been shown to significantly improve emotional intelligence. By utilizing tools such as calibration, anchoring, and reframing, individuals have been able to better understand their own emotions and those of others, leading to more empathetic and effective communication. For example, a study conducted in a corporate setting showed that employees who underwent NLP training demonstrated increased emotional awareness and better conflict resolution skills, resulting in a more harmonious and productive work environment. Similarly, in educational settings, incorporating NLP practices has led to improved student-teacher relationships and enhanced emotional regulation among students. These case studies highlight the transformative power of NLP in enhancing emotional intelligence and fostering positive interpersonal connections across various domains. The evidence presented underscores the potential of NLP as a valuable tool for personal growth and professional development.

XXVII. NLP AND COGNITIVE BEHAVIORAL TECHNIQUES

An integral aspect of NLP lies in its synergy with cognitive behavioral techniques, particularly in the realm of communication. By melding NLP principles with cognitive behavioral strategies, individuals can cultivate a more profound understanding of how thoughts, feelings, and behaviors intertwine to shape communication patterns. This fusion empowers individuals to not only decode the underlying dynamics of their interactions but also refine their responses to achieve more favorable outcomes. Through the incorporation of cognitive behavioral techniques, NLP practitioners can identify and challenge maladaptive thought patterns, reframe negative self-talk, and deploy effective communication strategies tailored to specific contexts. Ultimately, this convergence between NLP and cognitive behavioral techniques equips individuals with a comprehensive toolkit to navigate diverse communication scenarios with heightened awareness, empathy, and efficacy, thereby fostering more authentic and harmonious connections in both personal and professional spheres.

Comparing NLP with CBT

NLP and CBT are two powerful tools aimed at enhancing communication and promoting personal growth and change. While both approaches focus on transforming thought patterns and behaviors, they do so in different ways. NLP places a strong emphasis on the language we use and how it shapes our perceptions and interactions with the world. By exploring the connection between language, emotions, and behavior, NLP techniques can help individuals reframe negative thought patterns, build rapport, and improve communication skills. On the other hand, CBT is rooted in the belief that our thoughts influence our feelings and actions. Through structured interventions, CBT aims to identify and challenge distorted thinking patterns to bring about positive behavioral changes. While NLP and CBT share common goals of promoting personal growth and change, their methodologies and underlying principles set them apart. By understanding the nuances of each approach, individuals can choose the one that best suits their needs and goals.

Integrative approaches using NLP and CBT

One effective approach to enhancing communication skills is through the integration of NLP and CBT. By combining the principles of NLP, which focuses on understanding the relationship between language, behavior, and thought patterns, with the techniques of CBT, which emphasize changing negative thinking patterns to improve emotional responses, individuals can develop a more comprehensive and holistic approach to communication. Integrating NLP and CBT allows individuals to not only recognize and interpret both verbal and non-verbal cues more effectively but also to reframe negative beliefs and behaviors that may be affecting their communication style. This integrated approach empowers individuals to build stronger rapport, communicate more authentically, and achieve better outcomes in various social and professional settings. By blending the tools and strategies of NLP and CBT, individuals can enhance their communication skills and foster more positive and productive relationships.

Benefits of combining NLP with other psychological methods

The integration of NLP with other psychological methods can offer a wide range of benefits. By combining NLP techniques with approaches such as cognitive-behavioral therapy or psychoanalysis, individuals can access a more comprehensive toolkit for personal growth and development. For example, the use of NLP alongside mindfulness practices can enhance self-awareness and emotional regulation, leading to improved mental well-being. Additionally, incorporating NLP strategies into coaching or counseling sessions can help clients set and achieve concrete goals, overcome limiting beliefs, and cultivate a more positive mindset. The synergy between NLP and other psychological modalities can create a holistic approach to addressing various issues, providing individuals with a more tailored and effective path towards personal transformation and improved communication skills. This integration broadens the scope of possibilities for individuals seeking to enhance their interpersonal relationships, professional success, and overall well-being.

XXVIII. NLP IN MULTICULTURAL CONTEXTS

As individuals navigate the complex web of multicultural interactions, the application of NLP can play a pivotal role in bridging communication gaps and fostering understanding. In multicultural contexts, where diverse beliefs, values, and communication styles converge, NLP techniques offer a valuable toolkit for enhancing cross-cultural communication. By utilizing strategies such as mirroring, matching, and pacing, individuals can establish rapport and build trust with individuals from different cultural backgrounds. Moreover, the principles of NLP can empower individuals to effectively navigate cultural nuances, address potential misunderstandings, and adapt their communication style to resonate with multicultural audiences. In a globalized world where cultural sensitivity and effective communication are paramount, integrating NLP in multicultural contexts can serve as a powerful tool for promoting harmony, collaboration, and mutual respect among diverse communities.

Adapting NLP techniques for diverse cultures

As global communication continues to expand, the need to adapt NLP techniques for diverse cultures becomes increasingly important. NLP, with its focus on understanding and utilizing language patterns, behaviors, and beliefs, offers a powerful framework for enhancing communication across cultural boundaries. By tailoring NLP techniques to different cultural contexts, individuals can bridge the gap between varying communication styles, norms, and values. This adaptation involves not just translating NLP concepts into different languages, but also recognizing and respecting the nuances of different cultural expressions and interpretations. Understanding cultural diversity within the framework of NLP allows practitioners to communicate more effectively, build stronger connections, and avoid misunderstandings that may arise from cultural differences. Adapting NLP techniques for diverse cultures ultimately promotes inclusivity, empathy, and mutual understanding in communication practices, fostering more harmonious relationships and fruitful interactions across a wide range of cultural backgrounds.

Challenges of cross-cultural communication

One of the significant challenges of cross-cultural communication lies in the differences in non-verbal cues and gestures across different cultures. These subtle signs, such as eye contact, facial expressions, and body language, can vary greatly in their meanings from one culture to another, leading to misunderstandings and misinterpretations. Moreover, language barriers, varying communication styles, and cultural norms can further complicate intercultural interactions. Miscommunications can easily occur when individuals are unaware of these differences, hindering the effectiveness of communication and leading to conflict or unsuccessful outcomes. To overcome these challenges, individuals must cultivate cultural competence, empathy, and a willingness to learn and adapt to different communication styles. By embracing diversity, actively listening, and seeking to understand the perspectives of others, individuals can navigate cross-cultural communication with greater ease and effectiveness, fostering mutual respect and collaboration across cultural boundaries.

Success stories of NLP in multicultural settings

In multicultural settings, the successful implementation of NLP techniques has been demonstrated through various success stories. For instance, in a corporate environment where diverse teams collaborate, NLP has been utilized to enhance cross-cultural communication and foster understanding among team members from different backgrounds. By applying NLP tools such as mirroring and matching, individuals can establish rapport more effectively and bridge cultural gaps. Furthermore, in therapy sessions with clients from diverse cultural backgrounds, practitioners have found that NLP techniques assist in overcoming language barriers and building trust. Through the use of NLP strategies like meta-modeling and reframing, therapists have successfully guided clients to reframe their perspectives and achieve positive outcomes in their personal development journeys. These success stories highlight the transformative power of NLP in promoting effective communication and building harmonious relationships in multicultural contexts.

XXIX. NLP AND LANGUAGE LEARNING

In the context of NLP and language learning, it becomes evident that the principles and techniques of NLP can greatly enhance the process of acquiring a new language. By understanding how individuals process and interpret language, NLP tools such as modeling and meta-programs can be leveraged to optimize language learning strategies. Through the application of NLP, learners can gain insights into their own learning preferences and patterns, allowing them to tailor their study methods accordingly. Additionally, techniques such as reframing can help individuals overcome mental barriers and limiting beliefs that may hinder their language learning progress. By incorporating NLP principles into language learning curricula, educators can facilitate a more efficient and effective learning experience for students, ultimately leading to improved language proficiency and communication skills. The integration of NLP methodologies in language learning holds great potential for revolutionizing traditional language acquisition methods and fostering a deeper understanding and mastery of foreign languages.

Enhancing language acquisition through NLP

NLP offers a powerful framework for enhancing language acquisition by tapping into the connection between neurology, language, and behavior. By utilizing NLP techniques, individuals can improve their ability to understand and communicate more effectively in various contexts. Through techniques such as calibration, anchoring, and reframing, individuals can learn to decipher verbal and non-verbal cues, build rapport, and influence others positively. These tools are particularly useful for leaders, educators, therapists, and anyone looking to overcome communication barriers. Case studies and practical examples serve to illustrate the real-world application of NLP in enhancing language acquisition and fostering clearer, more persuasive communication. By embracing NLP principles, individuals can not only enhance their linguistic skills but also develop a more mindful and effective approach to interpersonal interactions. Overall, NLP offers a valuable toolkit for individuals seeking to strengthen their communication abilities and cultivate more meaningful relationships.

NLP strategies for language teachers and learners

NLP offers language teachers and learners a myriad of strategies to enhance their communication skills. By incorporating NLP techniques into their teaching methodologies, educators can create a more engaging and immersive learning environment for their students. Techniques such as mirroring and matching can help teachers establish better rapport with their students, leading to improved understanding and retention of information. For language learners, NLP can provide valuable tools for overcoming language barriers and improving their ability to communicate effectively in a new language. By utilizing NLP strategies such as anchoring and reframing, learners can enhance their language learning experience and accelerate their progress. Overall, NLP offers a unique and powerful approach to language teaching and learning that can benefit both teachers and students alike.

Examples of improved language skills via NLP techniques

As individuals begin to incorporate NLP techniques into their daily interactions, the results speak for themselves. Improved language skills are evident in various contexts, showcasing the transformative power of NLP. For instance, in professional settings, executives have reported increased success in negotiations and presentations through the utilization of anchoring techniques to evoke desired emotions in their audience. Additionally, educators have seen a marked improvement in student engagement by implementing reframing methods to shift perspectives and motivate learners. In therapeutic settings, clients have found breakthroughs in communication and self-awareness through calibration practices, leading to more profound and effective sessions. These examples underscore the versatility and impact of NLP techniques in enhancing language skills and fostering better understanding and connection between individuals. Ultimately, the application of NLP techniques showcases the potential for personal growth and improved relationships through more intentional and effective communication strategies.

XXX. NLP AND HEALTH COMMUNICATION

The utilization of NLP in the context of health communication represents a dynamic and innovative approach to enhancing patient-provider interactions and improving health outcomes. By incorporating NLP techniques such as mirroring, pacing, and leading, healthcare professionals can establish stronger connections with their patients, leading to increased trust, improved compliance with treatment plans, and better overall health outcomes. Moreover, NLP can also be applied in health education settings to enhance the delivery of complex information in a more accessible and engaging manner. By paying attention to the language used, as well as non-verbal cues, health educators can tailor their communication strategies to resonate with diverse audiences and facilitate better understanding. Overall, the integration of NLP principles in health communication holds great promise for fostering more effective and empathetic interactions within healthcare settings, ultimately benefiting both providers and patients alike.

Application of NLP in health care settings

NLP has been increasingly applied in health care settings to enhance patient-provider communication, improve treatment outcomes, and promote holistic healing. By utilizing NLP techniques such as mirroring, pacing, and leading, healthcare professionals can establish stronger connections with patients, build trust, and create a more empathetic environment. Through active listening and effective questioning, providers can better understand the needs and concerns of their patients, leading to more personalized and effective care plans. Additionally, NLP can be used to help patients overcome anxiety, manage pain, and improve their overall well-being through techniques such as visualization and positive reframing. By integrating NLP principles into healthcare practice, practitioners can not only improve patient satisfaction but also empower individuals to take an active role in their health and healing process. Ultimately, the application of NLP in health care settings holds great promise for enhancing the quality of care and fostering positive patient outcomes.

NLP techniques for patient communication

The application of NLP techniques in patient communication has shown significant promise in enhancing healthcare interactions. By utilizing NLP strategies such as mirroring, pacing, and leading, healthcare professionals can establish better rapport with patients, ultimately leading to improved patient satisfaction and treatment outcomes. These techniques enable practitioners to better understand patients' perspectives, communicate empathy, and create a supportive environment for shared decision-making. Additionally, tools like reframing can help healthcare providers address challenging situations or deliver difficult news in a more compassionate and effective manner. Through the integration of NLP principles into patient communication practices, healthcare professionals can cultivate a more positive and collaborative relationship with their patients, ultimately fostering better health outcomes and patient experiences.

Impact of NLP on health outcomes

As individuals strive to enhance their communication skills, the impact of NLP on health outcomes becomes increasingly relevant. By understanding how language patterns and non-verbal cues affect interpersonal interactions, individuals can improve their ability to convey empathy, build trust, and foster positive relationships. NLP techniques such as reframing can help individuals reframe negative thoughts or emotions that may be impacting their mental health, leading to improved well-being and overall quality of life. Additionally, the use of anchoring techniques in NLP can assist individuals in managing stress, anxiety, and other mental health challenges by creating positive triggers or associations to promote relaxation and emotional regulation. Ultimately, by incorporating NLP strategies into healthcare settings, practitioners can enhance patient communication, increase treatment adherence, and ultimately improve health outcomes for individuals.

XXXI. NLP AND NEGOTIATION SKILLS

NLP techniques are not only beneficial in enhancing communication skills but can also significantly impact negotiation abilities. By understanding and applying NLP principles, individuals can become more adept at reading verbal and non-verbal cues during negotiations, allowing them to adjust their approach for better outcomes. Techniques such as mirroring, pacing, and leading can help establish rapport with the other party, fostering a more collaborative atmosphere conducive to reaching mutually beneficial agreements. Moreover, NLP tools like reframing can help shift perspectives and encourage creative problem-solving during negotiations, leading to more innovative solutions. By incorporating NLP into negotiation strategies, individuals can not only improve their communication skills but also increase their effectiveness in bargaining, conflict resolution, and decision-making processes. As such, the integration of NLP and negotiation skills can be a powerful combination for achieving successful outcomes in various professional and personal contexts.

NLP strategies for effective negotiation

By incorporating NLP strategies into negotiation techniques, individuals can significantly enhance their effectiveness in achieving mutually beneficial outcomes. Understanding the power of language and the impact of non-verbal cues in communication is key to successful negotiation. Utilizing techniques such as mirroring, pacing, and leading can help establish rapport and create a sense of connection with the other party. Moreover, employing the principles of calibration can enable negotiators to adapt their communication style based on the feedback received, allowing for greater flexibility and responsiveness during the negotiation process. By anchoring positive associations and reframing challenges as opportunities, negotiators can also influence the perception and mindset of the other party, ultimately fostering a more collaborative and constructive negotiation environment. These NLP strategies offer a comprehensive toolkit for improving negotiation skills and fostering more meaningful and productive interactions in various contexts.

Role of language patterns in negotiation

The role of language patterns in negotiation cannot be understated when considering the intricacies of effective communication. Language serves as a powerful tool in shaping perceptions, establishing rapport, and influencing outcomes in negotiations. Words have the ability to build trust, establish common ground, and convey complex ideas in a succinct manner. Moreover, the choice of language patterns can impact the tone and direction of a negotiation, either fostering cooperation or intensifying conflict. By employing the principles of NLP , negotiators can strategically use language to establish a positive emotional connection, influence decision-making processes, and navigate potential obstacles with finesse. Through an understanding of how language patterns can shape interactions, individuals can enhance their negotiation skills, cultivate better relationships, and achieve mutually beneficial outcomes. The art of negotiation lies in not only what is said, but how it is said, demonstrating the significant role language patterns play in successful communication and conflict resolution.

Case studies of successful negotiations using NLP

The exploration of successful negotiations using NLP reveals the transformative impact of NLP techniques on communication dynamics. By delving into case studies of individuals who have effectively applied NLP principles to their negotiation strategies, a clear pattern emerges. In these cases, practitioners have been able to establish strong rapport, accurately calibrate the responses of their counterparts, and skillfully reframe challenges into opportunities for mutual benefit. These examples illuminate the power of NLP in fostering understanding, trust, and collaboration during high-stakes negotiations. By utilizing anchoring techniques to influence emotional states and reframing language to reshape perspectives, negotiators have achieved remarkable results in diverse settings. These case studies serve as compelling evidence of NLP's effectiveness in enhancing communication skills and achieving positive outcomes in complex negotiations.

XXXII. NLP AND CUSTOMER SERVICE

The integration of NLP techniques in customer service can revolutionize the way businesses interact with their clients. By understanding the power of language, tonality, and body language, customer service representatives can build strong rapport with customers, leading to increased customer satisfaction and loyalty. NLP tools such as mirroring and matching can help establish a deeper connection with clients, allowing representatives to tailor their communication style to better meet the needs of the customer. Moreover, the ability to reframe situations can turn potentially negative customer interactions into positive experiences, showcasing the importance of effective communication in diffusing tense situations. When applied effectively, NLP in customer service can not only enhance the overall customer experience but also improve employee satisfaction and productivity, creating a win-win situation for both the business and its clientele.

Improving customer interactions with NLP

In today's fast-paced and technology-driven world, enhancing customer interactions is paramount for businesses aiming to build strong relationships and drive loyalty. One effective way to achieve this is through the use of NLP techniques. By leveraging NLP tools, businesses can gain valuable insights into customer sentiments, preferences, and needs, enabling them to tailor their interactions in a more personalized and meaningful way. NLP can help businesses analyze vast amounts of customer data, extract valuable information, and generate actionable insights to improve customer service and satisfaction. Additionally, NLP can facilitate faster response times, automate processes, and provide real-time support to customers, ultimately leading to a more seamless and efficient customer experience. By incorporating NLP into customer interactions, businesses can not only enhance communication but also foster stronger connections with their customers, driving long-term success and growth.

NLP techniques for customer satisfaction

In the realm of customer satisfaction, NLP techniques hold immense potential for businesses seeking to enhance their communication strategies. By incorporating NLP principles into customer interactions, companies can better understand customers' needs and preferences, leading to improved overall satisfaction. Techniques such as mirroring, pacing, and matching can help build rapport with customers, fostering a sense of trust and understanding. Additionally, utilizing NLP methods like reframing can assist in resolving potential conflicts or misunderstandings, ultimately leading to more positive outcomes for both parties involved. By implementing these NLP tools effectively, businesses can create a more personalized and engaging experience for their customers, paving the way for increased loyalty and repeat business. Overall, the application of NLP techniques in customer interactions has the potential to transform the landscape of customer satisfaction and relationship management in today's competitive market.

Examples of enhanced customer service through NLP

In the realm of customer service, NLP has proven to be a valuable tool for enhancing interactions and building strong relationships with clients. One example of how NLP can improve customer service is through the use of mirroring and matching techniques. By subtly mirroring a customer's body language, tone of voice, or key phrases, a service agent can establish rapport and create a sense of connection. This can lead to increased trust and improved communication, ultimately enhancing the overall customer experience. Additionally, NLP techniques such as pacing and leading can be used to guide customers through difficult conversations or to help them see things from a different perspective. By employing NLP strategies effectively, businesses can not only resolve customer issues more efficiently but also create a positive and memorable experience that fosters customer loyalty and satisfaction.

XXXIII. NLP AND ORGANIZATIONAL DEVELOPMENT

NLP offers valuable tools for organizational development by enhancing communication within business settings. Through techniques like calibration, anchoring, and reframing, leaders can gain a deeper understanding of their team members' perspectives and motivations. By utilizing NLP in organizational contexts, managers can build rapport, resolve conflicts, and inspire teamwork. Case studies demonstrate how NLP has been successfully implemented in various industries to improve employee engagement and productivity. Furthermore, NLP can help organizations adapt to change more effectively by fostering a culture of open communication and flexibility. By integrating NLP practices into leadership development programs, companies can create a more cohesive and resilient workforce. Ultimately, NLP can be a powerful tool for organizational growth and success in today's rapidly evolving business landscape.

NLP's role in organizational change

As organizations strive to navigate the complexities of an ever-evolving business landscape, the role of NLP in facilitating organizational change cannot be understated. NLP techniques offer a powerful framework for enhancing communication, fostering empathy, and driving positive transformation within teams and across departments. By utilizing NLP tools such as language patterns, perceptual positions, and meta-modeling, leaders can effectively communicate visions, inspire motivation, and promote a culture of collaboration and innovation. A key aspect of

NLP's impact on organizational change lies in its ability to uncover underlying beliefs, values, and attitudes that may be hindering progress or fostering resistance to change. Through targeted interventions and strategic interventions, NLP can help leaders overcome communication barriers, build trust, and create a more conducive environment for successful change initiatives. Embracing NLP within organizations can lead to improved employee engagement, enhanced performance, and sustainable growth in today's dynamic business environment.

Techniques for organizational communication improvement

In the quest for enhancing organizational communication, the utilization of NLP techniques has emerged as a powerful tool. By delving into concepts such as calibration, anchoring, and reframing, individuals can fine-tune their communication skills to build stronger connections and convey their messages more effectively. Through the careful application of these techniques, organizational leaders can create a more cohesive and productive work environment, where team members feel heard and valued. Moreover, NLP strategies can help improve conflict resolution, negotiation, and overall decision-making processes within the organization. By incorporating NLP techniques into their communication repertoire, individuals can not only enhance their own effectiveness but also contribute to a more positive and harmonious organizational culture. Ultimately, mastering these techniques can lead to improved relationships, increased productivity, and overall success within the organizational context.

Case studies of organizational development using NLP

Organizational development using NLP has been a topic of interest for many researchers and practitioners seeking to enhance communication and effectiveness within their respective organizations. Case studies have shown how NLP techniques can be successfully applied to address specific challenges and achieve desired outcomes. For instance, a case study in a corporate setting may demonstrate how NLP tools like metaprograms and meta-modeling can help leaders understand and motivate their team members more effectively. By applying these techniques, organizations can improve employee engagement, increase productivity, and foster a more positive work culture. These case studies serve as valuable examples of the practical implementation of NLP principles in real-world scenarios, providing insights into the transformative power of NLP in organizational contexts. As more organizations recognize the benefits of using NLP for organizational development, these case studies will continue to offer valuable insights and inspiration for others looking to apply NLP techniques in their own workplace environments.

XXXIV. NLP AND PERSONAL DEVELOPMENT

By integrating NLP techniques into personal development, individuals can gain invaluable tools for enhancing their communication skills and achieving personal growth. NLP offers a comprehensive framework for understanding and improving how we interact with others, both verbally and non-verbally. Concepts like calibration, anchoring, and reframing provide practical strategies for building rapport, resolving conflicts, and influencing others positively. Through the application of NLP techniques, individuals can overcome communication barriers, develop a deeper sense of empathy, and foster stronger relationships in all areas of life. This holistic approach to personal development not only enhances one's communication abilities but also encourages self-reflection and mindfulness in interactions. By incorporating NLP principles into daily practices, individuals can cultivate more effective communication habits, leading to greater personal fulfillment and success. In this way, NLP serves as a powerful tool for personal growth and transformation.

Self-improvement through NLP techniques

NLP offers a powerful toolkit for self-improvement, enhancing communication skills, and fostering personal growth. By delving into the techniques of NLP, individuals can gain a deeper understanding of their own thought patterns, behaviors, and language use. Through practices such as visualization, reframing negative beliefs, and setting achievable goals, NLP empowers individuals to break free from limiting beliefs and cultivate a more positive mindset. The utilization of NLP techniques can lead to heightened self-awareness, improved interpersonal relationships, and increased effectiveness in various areas of life. Moreover, NLP provides strategies for managing stress, overcoming obstacles, and achieving personal success. By incorporating NLP practices into daily routines, individuals can tap into their full potential, cultivate resilience, and create meaningful change in their lives. Thus, self-improvement through NLP techniques can pave the way for personal transformation and enhanced well-being.

NLP for goal setting and personal growth

As individuals strive for personal growth and strive to attain their goals, NLP emerges as a valuable tool to navigate the complexities of the human mind and behavior. By utilizing NLP techniques for goal setting, individuals can enhance self-awareness, clarify their objectives, and establish an effective roadmap for progress. NLP provides a framework for identifying limiting beliefs, reframing negative thought patterns, and cultivating a positive mindset conducive to growth and success. Through techniques such as visualization, modeling, and setting well-formed outcomes, individuals can create a clear vision of their goals and take actionable steps towards achieving them. NLP also emphasizes the power of language and communication in shaping our reality, encouraging individuals to use empowering language, set SMART (Specific, Measurable, Achievable, Relevant, Time-bound) goals, and leverage the power of persuasion to influence themselves and others positively. In essence, NLP serves as a powerful ally in the journey towards personal development, offering a profound understanding of the subconscious mind and the tools to harness its potential for transformative change.

Success stories of personal transformation with NLP

In the realm of personal transformation, NLP has generated numerous success stories showcasing its efficacy in fostering positive change. By honing in on key elements such as calibration, anchoring, and reframing, individuals have been able to reframe their mindset and behavior, paving the way for significant personal growth. For instance, leaders have utilized NLP techniques to enhance communication with their teams, resulting in improved collaboration and productivity. Educators have leveraged NLP to better connect with students, creating a conducive learning environment. Therapists have employed NLP strategies to help clients break through self-limiting beliefs and achieve breakthroughs in their mental health journey. These anecdotes underscore the versatility and power of NLP in facilitating profound transformations, proving its effectiveness in various contexts. Through these success stories, individuals are inspired to harness the tools of NLP to actualize their potential and cultivate meaningful change in their lives.

XXXV. NLP AND SPORTS COACHING

As NLP continues to gain recognition for its profound impact on communication strategies, its application in the realm of sports coaching is becoming increasingly prevalent. Coaches are finding that the principles of NLP can be invaluable in improving athlete performance, enhancing team dynamics, and fostering a winning mindset. By leveraging techniques such as language patterns, mirroring, and perceptual positions, coaches can effectively communicate with athletes, motivate them to achieve their full potential, and facilitate mental resilience in the face of adversity. Furthermore, NLP tools like visualization and goal setting can aid in enhancing athletes' focus, confidence, and overall mental toughness. Through the integration of NLP into sports coaching, a new frontier of understanding and optimizing human performance is being explored, opening up possibilities for athletes and teams to reach new heights in their competitive endeavors.

Application of NLP in sports psychology

NLP has found a valuable application in the field of sports psychology, where it can significantly impact athletes' performance and mental well-being. By harnessing NLP techniques, sports psychologists can help athletes overcome mental barriers, improve focus, and enhance their overall mindset. Techniques such as visualization, anchoring, and reframing can aid athletes in boosting their confidence, managing stress, and achieving peak performance levels. Through NLP, athletes can develop a stronger sense of self-awareness, set effective goals, and culti-vate a winning mentality. Moreover, NLP can facilitate better communication between coaches and athletes, fostering a supportive and constructive relationship essential for athletic success. Ultimately, the strategic application of NLP in sports psychology not only enhances performance but also contributes to athletes' overall psychological resilience and well-being.

Techniques for enhancing athletic performance

In the realm of athletic performance enhancement, various techniques have been developed to help athletes reach their full potential. One such technique is visualization, where athletes mentally rehearse their desired outcomes in intricate detail, creating a powerful mind-body connection. Additionally, goal setting plays a crucial role in improving performance by providing athletes with a clear direction and motivation to push themselves beyond their limits. Another effective technique is the use of positive self-talk, which helps athletes cultivate a strong mindset and boost their confidence levels. Moreover, incorporating proper nutrition and hydration practices can optimize physical performance and recovery, allowing athletes to sustain peak performance levels. Overall, by employing a combination of these techniques, athletes can enhance their performance, achieve their goals, and excel in their respective sports.

Examples of NLP in professional sports coaching

NLP has found applications in professional sports coaching, revolutionizing the way athletes and coaches communicate and perform. By utilizing NLP techniques, coaches can better understand the mindset of their athletes, tailor their feedback to individual learning styles, and motivate them effectively. For example, using anchoring techniques, coaches can help athletes enter a state of peak performance by associating specific mental cues with optimal physical and emotional states. Through reframing, coaches can help athletes shift their perspective on challenges, turning setbacks into learning opportunities. Additionally, calibration enables coaches to read subtle cues in body language and tone of voice, allowing them to make real-time adjustments to their coaching approach. Overall, the integration of NLP in professional sports coaching has proven to enhance athlete-coach relationships, improve performance, and contribute to a more successful and fulfilling experience for all involved.

XXXVI. NLP AND CREATIVITY

One significant aspect of NLP that has garnered attention is its relationship with creativity. By enhancing communication skills, NLP can unlock an individual's creative potential and facilitate the generation of innovative ideas. Through techniques like reframing, individuals can view situations from different perspectives, fostering a more open-minded approach to problem-solving and idea generation. Anchoring techniques can also be used to access resourceful states, boosting confidence and stimulating creative thinking. Additionally, NLP aids in building strong rapport with others, creating a supportive environment where creativity can flourish through collaboration and shared ideas. By incorporating NLP principles into the creative process, individuals can tap into their subconscious minds, unleash their creativity, and harness the power of effective communication to bring their ideas to life. In this way, NLP serves as a valuable tool for enhancing creativity and innovation in various domains.

Enhancing creative processes through NLP

As individuals strive to enhance their creative processes, NLP emerges as a powerful tool for unlocking untapped potential. By understanding how language and perception influence thought patterns, practitioners can reshape the way they approach problems and generate innovative solutions. NLP techniques provide a framework for breaking through mental barriers, promoting flexibility in thinking, and fostering a more open-minded approach to creativity. Through the practice of anchoring positive experiences, reframing limiting beliefs, and fine-tuning communication skills, individuals can cultivate a mindset conducive to creativity and innovation. By integrating NLP into daily practices, individuals can harness the power of their subconscious mind, tap into their creativity, and unleash a wealth of innovative ideas. Ultimately, by enhancing creative processes through NLP, individuals can navigate challenges with greater insight, adaptability, and a heightened sense of imagination.

NLP techniques for creative thinking

NLP techniques offer a unique and innovative approach to fostering creative thinking. By tapping into the power of language, imagery, and sensory perception, individuals can effectively break through mental barriers and unleash their creative potential. Utilizing techniques such as modeling, reframing, and sensory acuity, NLP provides a framework for enhancing cognitive flexibility and expanding problem-solving capabilities. Through the practice of visualization and metaphorical thinking, individuals can generate novel ideas, think outside the box, and approach challenges from a fresh perspective. Additionally, NLP techniques can be used to enhance collaboration and brainstorming processes, fostering a creative and synergistic work environment. By incorporating NLP practices into their repertoire, individuals can cultivate a more innovative mindset, leading to increased adaptability, resilience, and creativity in both professional and personal endeavors.

Case studies of creativity improvement using NLP

In studying the application of NLP for creativity improvement, a number of intriguing case studies have emerged. These cases showcase how individuals across various fields have effectively harnessed NLP techniques to enhance their creative capacities. By using NLP methods such as modeling excellence, reframing limiting beliefs, and utilizing sensory acuity, these individuals were able to break through creative blocks, generate fresh ideas, and approach challenges from new perspectives. For instance, a graphic designer struggling with creative stagnation found renewed inspiration by applying NLP techniques to shift her mindset and tap into her innate creativity. Similarly, a software developer was able to enhance his problem-solving skills by using NLP to reframe obstacles as opportunities for innovation. These case studies highlight the transformative power of NLP in fostering creativity and unlocking new levels of innovation.

XXXVII. NLP AND CONFLICT MANAGEMENT

As the intricate world of NLP unfolds within the pages of this book, one particularly intriguing application emerges in the realm of conflict management. In this chapter, the synergistic relationship between NLP techniques and conflict resolution strategies is elucidated. By honing the skills of active listening, empathetic communication, and understanding behavioral patterns, individuals can utilize NLP to navigate tense situations with finesse and sensitivity. Through the lens of NLP, conflict is reframed not as a battle to be won, but as an opportunity for mutual understanding and growth. Techniques such as mirroring, pacing, and leading can be employed to establish rapport and defuse hostilities, paving the way for constructive dialogue and resolution. By empowering individuals to decode the underlying motivations and dynamics at play in conflicts, NLP equips them with the tools to foster harmony, build trust, and cultivate stronger relationships in both personal and professional spheres.

NLP strategies for managing interpersonal conflicts

NLP offers a variety of strategies for effectively managing interpersonal conflicts. By utilizing techniques such as mirroring and matching, individuals can establish a sense of rapport and connection with others, laying the foundation for constructive dialogue. Additionally, the concept of reframing is instrumental in shifting perspectives and finding common ground in contentious situations. Through NLP, individuals can gain insight into their own communication patterns and learn to adjust their behavior to promote understanding and resolution. By identifying and addressing underlying beliefs and values, NLP techniques can help navigate conflicts with empathy and clarity, leading to more harmonious relationships and successful outcomes. Ultimately, by integrating NLP strategies into conflict management practices, individuals can cultivate a deeper level of communication and collaboration in various social and professional contexts.

Techniques for effective conflict mediation

When considering techniques for effective conflict mediation within the realm of NLP , it is crucial to understand the power of reframing in shifting perspectives and finding common ground. By encouraging individuals engaged in conflict to reframe their understanding of the situation, NLP practitioners can help them see the issue from different angles and identify potential solutions collaboratively. Additionally, anchoring techniques can be utilized to de-escalate tense situations and redirect emotions towards a more constructive dialogue. Through the use of anchors, such as calming words or gestures, mediators can guide conflicted parties towards a state of calmness and receptivity, fostering a conducive environment for resolution. Moreover, calibration plays a fundamental role in conflict mediation by enabling practitioners to read and interpret the subtle cues and signals emitted by individuals in conflict, allowing for a deeper understanding of their underlying emotions and needs. By incorporating these NLP techniques into conflict mediation practices, individuals can cultivate effective communication strategies and facilitate the resolution of conflicts in a more harmonious and sustainable manner.

Examples of conflict resolution through NLP

Examples of conflict resolution through NLP showcase the power of language and perception in diffusing tense situations and fostering understanding. By utilizing techniques such as mirroring and matching, individuals can establish rapport and empathy, creating a conducive atmosphere for resolving disputes. For instance, a manager dealing with a conflict between two team members can employ NLP strategies to align their communication styles, identify common ground, and facilitate a constructive dialogue. Moreover, reframing negative interpretations or beliefs can help shift perspectives and promote mutual respect, ultimately leading to a more harmonious resolution. Through NLP, individuals can not only address conflict efficiently but also cultivate stronger relationships based on trust, empathy, and effective communication. These examples highlight the transformative potential of NLP in navigating interpersonal challenges and fostering collaborative solutions.

XXXVIII. NLP AND DECISION MAKING

In the realm of NLP, decision-making processes can be significantly enhanced through the application of various techniques and strategies. By leveraging NLP principles, individuals can develop a deeper understanding of their own cognitive patterns and biases, allowing them to make more informed and rational decisions. Techniques such as anchoring and reframing can help individuals overcome limiting beliefs or emotional barriers that may impede effective decision-making. Moreover, NLP can aid in improving communication skills, which are essential for navigating complex decision-making scenarios. Through the cultivation of rapport-building skills and the ability to accurately interpret verbal and non-verbal cues, individuals can enhance their ability to influence outcomes and make decisions that align with their goals and values. Overall, the integration of NLP into the decision-making process offers a powerful framework for enhancing cognitive clarity and effectiveness in navigating the complexities of modern life.

Improving decision-making skills with NLP

NLP offers a powerful toolkit for enhancing decision-making skills by providing individuals with the ability to understand and influence their own thought processes. By utilizing techniques like reframing and anchoring, individuals can reframe their perspectives on various situations and anchor positive emotions to specific triggers, thus enabling them to make more informed and effective decisions. NLP also helps individuals recognize and address limiting beliefs and unconscious biases that may hinder their decision-making abilities, ultimately leading to more confident and rational choices. Through the exploration and application of NLP principles, individuals can develop a deeper awareness of their cognitive patterns and improve their ability to make decisions that align with their goals and values. By honing these skills, individuals can navigate complex and challenging situations with clarity and purpose, ultimately enhancing their overall success and well-being.

NLP techniques for clearer thinking

The integration of NLP techniques into our cognitive processes can significantly enhance clarity of thought. By utilizing strategies such as calibration, anchoring, and reframing, individuals can gain a deeper understanding of their own thoughts and emotions, leading to more coherent and rational decision-making. NLP emphasizes the importance of paying attention to both verbal and non-verbal cues, allowing individuals to better interpret and respond to various forms of communication. Through case studies and practical examples, it becomes evident how these techniques can be effectively applied in diverse situations, from leadership roles to personal relationships. By implementing NLP principles, individuals can refine their thought processes, mitigate cognitive biases, and foster more effective communication with others. Ultimately, the mastery of NLP techniques offers a pathway to clearer thinking and enhanced mental acuity in all facets of life.

Case studies of decision-making enhancement using NLP

NLP has been utilized in various case studies to enhance decision-making processes. By leveraging NLP techniques, individuals have been able to improve their ability to interpret and respond to different situations effectively. For instance, through the use of strategies like reframing and anchoring, leaders have been able to make more informed choices in high-pressure environments. Educators have also found NLP beneficial in understanding students' learning preferences and adapting their teaching methods accordingly. Furthermore, therapists have used NLP to help patients overcome cognitive biases and make healthier decisions. These case studies highlight the versatility of NLP in enhancing decision-making across diverse fields, emphasizing its role in fostering clearer communication, better relationships, and more successful outcomes. By studying these real-world examples, individuals can gain insights into the practical applications of NLP and its potential to transform decision-making processes for the better.

XXXIX. NLP AND STRESS MANAGEMENT

In the realm of stress management, NLP offers a powerful set of tools and techniques that can help individuals navigate and alleviate stressors effectively. By utilizing techniques such as reframing negative experiences, building anchors that evoke positive emotions, and calibrating one's own responses to stressful situations, NLP empowers individuals to take control of their reactions and mindset. Through the practice of NLP, individuals can develop a heightened sense of self-awareness, identify triggers that lead to stress, and cultivate strategies to manage and mitigate these triggers. By honing their communication skills using NLP principles, individuals can also improve their ability to convey their feelings, needs, and boundaries in a clear and assertive manner, reducing misunderstandings and conflicts that can contribute to elevated stress levels. Overall, the integration of NLP into stress management techniques can provide individuals with a comprehensive approach to cultivating resilience, emotional intelligence, and overall well-being.

NLP techniques for stress reduction

One notable application of NLP techniques is in the realm of stress reduction. By harnessing the power of NLP, individuals can learn to manage and alleviate stress by reprogramming their thought patterns and responses. One key NLP technique for stress reduction is visualization, where individuals are guided to create positive mental images that counteract negative emotions associated with stress. Additionally, NLP practices such as anchoring and reframing can help individuals shift their perspective on stressors and develop more adaptive coping mechanisms. Through the use of NLP techniques, individuals can develop a greater sense of self-awareness and control over their thoughts and emotions, ultimately leading to a reduction in stress levels and an improved overall well-being. By incorporating NLP into their daily routines, individuals can cultivate a more resilient mindset and better navigate the challenges presented by modern-day stressors.

Role of NLP in managing emotional stress

In the realm of managing emotional stress, NLP plays a vital role in providing individuals with tools and techniques to enhance their emotional well-being. By utilizing NLP strategies such as reframing negative thoughts, anchoring positive emotions, and implementing effective communication patterns, individuals can effectively manage and reduce emotional stress. Through the practice of NLP, individuals can gain a deeper understanding of their thought patterns and behaviors, leading to improved self-awareness and emotional regulation. NLP offers practical methods for shifting perspective, changing beliefs, and developing resilience in the face of challenging situations. By incorporating NLP into their daily routines, individuals can cultivate a more positive mindset, increase emotional intelligence, and ultimately experience greater emotional stability in their lives. Overall, NLP serves as a valuable tool for empowering individuals to navigate and overcome emotional stressors effectively.

Examples of stress management using NLP

By incorporating NLP techniques, individuals can effectively manage stress and improve their overall well-being. Utilizing techniques such as anchoring, individuals can create positive triggers that help them remain calm and focused during challenging situations. By learning how to reframe negative thought patterns, individuals can shift their perspective and reduce the impact of stressors. Additionally, practicing mindfulness and visualization techniques can help individuals stay present and maintain a sense of control in stressful situations. Through the use of NLP, individuals can develop better self-awareness and emotional regulation skills, allowing them to navigate stress more effectively. Ultimately, the integration of NLP into stress management strategies provides individuals with powerful tools to cultivate resilience, enhance their coping mechanisms, and improve their overall quality of life.

XL. NLP AND TEAM BUILDING

NLP offers a unique approach to team building by focusing on enhancing communication and understanding between team members. By integrating NLP techniques such as calibration, anchoring, and reframing, team leaders can foster a more cohesive and productive work environment. Through the process of calibration, team members can better tune into each other's verbal and non-verbal cues, leading to improved understanding and empathy. Anchoring allows team leaders to create positive associations within the team, reinforcing motivation and collaboration. Additionally, reframing enables team members to view challenges from different perspectives, promoting creative problem-solving and conflict resolution. Case studies and practical examples highlight how NLP tools can be effectively utilized to strengthen team dynamics and achieve collective goals, making NLP a valuable resource for enhancing teamwork in a variety of professional contexts. By incorporating NLP principles into team building strategies, organizations can cultivate a culture of effective communication, trust, and synergy among team members.

NLP strategies for effective team dynamics

When it comes to bolstering team dynamics, NLP offers a plethora of strategies that can be leveraged to enhance communication and collaboration. By utilizing techniques such as calibration, team members can tune into each other's non-verbal cues and build rapport more effectively. Anchoring can further strengthen team dynamics by creating positive associations

with past successes, fostering a sense of cohesion and motivation within the group. Additionally, reframing can help team members shift their perspectives on challenges, turning obstacles into opportunities for growth and innovation. Through the application of these NLP tools, teams can not only improve their communication but also cultivate a more harmonious and productive working environment. Ultimately, by integrating NLP strategies into team dynamics, organizations can unlock the full potential of their teams and achieve greater success in their endeavors.

Techniques for fostering team collaboration

Effective techniques for fostering team collaboration within an organization are crucial for achieving synergy and maximizing productivity. One method is through establishing clear communication channels that encourage open dialogue and idea-sharing among team members. By promoting active listening and feedback, individuals can feel valued and engaged, leading to a more cohesive and cooperative work environment. Additionally, cultivating a sense of trust and psychological safety within the team can foster a collaborative atmosphere where team members feel comfortable taking risks and sharing their perspectives without fear of judgment. Setting collective goals and objectives that align with each team member's strengths and expertise can also enhance collaboration by leveraging individual talents to achieve common objectives. Overall, by implementing these techniques, organizations can create a supportive and collaborative team culture that drives success and innovation.

Case studies of team development using NLP

An integral part of understanding the practical application of NLP lies in examining case studies of team development where NLP techniques have been utilized. These studies provide real-world examples of how NLP can be effectively implemented to enhance communication, foster collaboration, and drive positive outcomes within teams. By delving into these cases, researchers can gain valuable insights into the specific strategies and tools employed in various contexts, shedding light on the potential benefits and challenges associated with using NLP in team settings. Through a thorough analysis of these case studies, a deeper understanding of the nuances of NLP techniques and their impact on team dynamics can be achieved, offering a wealth of knowledge for practitioners and scholars alike. Ultimately, these case studies serve as a testament to the versatility and efficacy of NLP in facilitating team development and improving overall group performance.

XLI. NLP AND CHANGE MANAGEMENT

One area where NLP has shown significant impact is in the realm of change management. NLP techniques can be instrumental in facilitating successful change initiatives within organizations by addressing the psychological and emotional aspects of transformation. By leveraging NLP tools such as reframing, practitioners can help individuals within the organization perceive change in a more positive light, thereby reducing resistance and fostering a culture of adaptability. Anchoring techniques can also be used to associate change with positive emotions, reinforcing a sense of motivation and commitment among employees. Furthermore, NLP's focus on communication skills equips change leaders with the ability to effectively convey the rationale behind change initiatives, inspiring confidence and buy-in from stakeholders. Ultimately, the integration of NLP principles into change management strategies can lead to smoother transitions, higher levels of employee engagement, and greater overall success in organizational change efforts.

NLP's role in facilitating change

NLP serves as a powerful tool in facilitating change by enhancing communication skills and fostering personal growth. Through its techniques, individuals can gain a deeper understanding of how language and behavior are interconnected, enabling them to break free from limiting beliefs and patterns. By mastering NLP concepts such as calibration, anchoring, and reframing, individuals can develop a heightened awareness of their own communication styles and how they impact others. This heightened awareness allows for more effective interactions, the ability to build rapport, and the skill to influence others positively. Case studies and practical examples further highlight how NLP can be applied in various contexts to overcome barriers and achieve desired outcomes, making it a valuable resource for navigating the complexities of human communication and nurturing stronger interpersonal relationships. In essence, NLP empowers individuals to transform their communication patterns and create meaningful change in both professional and personal spheres.

Techniques for managing change in organizations

One effective technique for managing change in organizations is the concept of anchoring in NLP . Anchoring involves linking a particular emotional state or response to a specific trigger, such as a word, gesture, or visual cue. By establishing positive anchors related to change within an organization, leaders can help employees associate excitement, motivation, or optimism with the idea of change. This can create a more receptive and open-minded environment for transitioning to new processes, systems, or structures within the organization. Additionally, leaders can utilize calibration techniques to accurately assess the reactions and responses of employees to change, allowing for tailored and targeted interventions to address resistance or concerns. Overall, by applying NLP techniques like anchoring and calibration, organizations can effectively navigate and manage change while fostering a culture of agility and adaptability.

Examples of successful change management using NLP

The successful application of NLP in change management has been evident in various contexts, showcasing its effectiveness in facilitating transformation within organizations. For instance, a prominent tech company utilized NLP techniques to foster a culture of innovation and collaboration among its employees during a major restructuring process. Through the implementation of anchoring techniques and reframing strategies, leaders were able to alleviate resistance to change, enhance employee engagement, and drive successful adoption of new systems and processes. By effectively calibrating the communication styles of key stakeholders and leveraging NLP principles to build rapport and trust, the organization was able to navigate through complex transitions with agility and efficiency. These examples highlight the transformative power of NLP in driving organizational change and achieving desired outcomes in a dynamic and rapidly evolving business landscape.

XLII. NLP AND LIFE COACHING

An integral application of NLP techniques is within the realm of life coaching, where the principles of NLP can be harnessed to facilitate personal growth and development. By leveraging NLP strategies such as modeling excellence, setting well-formed outcomes, and utilizing language patterns for positive change, life coaches can empower individuals to overcome limiting beliefs, enhance self-awareness, and achieve their full potential. Through the establishment of rapport, active listening, and effective questioning, NLP-trained life coaches can guide clients towards clarity, goal-setting, and ultimately, transformation. These tools not only enable clients to navigate challenges and obstacles but also enhance their communicative skills, emotional intelligence, and overall well-being. The synergy between NLP and life coaching offers a potent combination for individuals seeking professional guidance and support in navigating the complexities of personal growth and self-discovery.

The role of NLP in life coaching

NLP has gained recognition in the field of life coaching as a powerful tool for enhancing communication skills and facilitating personal growth. By drawing on techniques such as calibration, anchoring, and reframing, NLP practitioners can help individuals identify and overcome limiting beliefs, set clear goals, and navigate challenges with a more resourceful mindset. In the context of life coaching, NLP serves as a valuable framework for fostering self-awareness, empowering clients to make positive changes, and improving their overall well-being. Through the lens of NLP, life coaches can guide clients in uncovering subconscious patterns, reframing negative thought patterns, and developing more effective strategies for achieving desired outcomes. Ultimately, the integration of NLP principles into life coaching practices can lead to transformative results, enabling clients to unlock their full potential and create meaningful changes in various areas of their lives.

Techniques for effective life coaching

NLP offers a range of techniques for effective life coaching that can significantly enhance interpersonal communication. Calibration, one of the core concepts of NLP, involves the ability to observe and perceive subtle cues in both verbal and non-verbal communication, allowing coaches to adjust their approach accordingly. Anchoring is another powerful technique that helps clients associate positive emotions with specific triggers, enabling them to access desired states of mind more easily. Additionally, reframing techniques in NLP can guide individuals in shifting their perspectives on challenging situations, empowering them to see things in a more positive light. By mastering these techniques, life coaches can build rapport, inspire motivation, and facilitate personal growth in their clients. When applied skillfully, NLP techniques can help individuals overcome barriers, achieve their goals, and cultivate more fulfilling relationships in both personal and professional realms.

Success stories of life coaching with NLP

One remarkable success story of life coaching with NLP involved a young professional who struggled with public speaking anxiety. Through NLP sessions, she learned to reframe her fear into excitement, transforming her mindset and improving her confidence on stage. By utilizing anchoring techniques, she was able to associate positive emotions with speaking opportunities, allowing her to deliver presentations with ease and grace. Additionally, the process of calibrating her body language and vocal tone helped her establish a strong connection with her audience, leading to greater engagement and impact. This case exemplifies how NLP can empower individuals to overcome limiting beliefs and achieve their full potential in various areas of life. Such success stories showcase the transformative power of life coaching with NLP in enhancing communication skills, boosting self-confidence, and fostering personal growth on a profound level.

XLIII. NLP AND CAREER DEVELOPMENT

NLP offers more than just tools for effective communication; it also holds significant benefits for career development. By mastering NLP techniques such as calibration, anchoring, and reframing, individuals can enhance their communication skills in professional settings. Understanding verbal and non-verbal cues can help navigate office dynamics, build rapport with colleagues, and present ideas more persuasively. Through case studies and practical examples, it becomes clear how NLP can be utilized by leaders, educators, and individuals seeking advancement in their careers. By adopting a mindful and effective approach to communication, one can not only improve interactions within the workplace but also increase opportunities for career growth and success. In essence, integrating NLP into career development strategies can lead to better relationships, heightened influence, and overall professional advancement.

NLP techniques for career advancement

By applying NLP techniques to career advancement, individuals can significantly enhance their communication skills and overall professional success. NLP provides tools such as calibration, anchoring, and reframing, which can help individuals better understand their own communication patterns and those of others. Through the practice of these techniques, individuals can build effective rapport with colleagues, clients, and stakeholders, leading to improved collaboration and influence in the workplace. Furthermore, by mastering NLP techniques, individuals can navigate challenging conversations with confidence and clarity, ultimately positioning themselves for career growth and development. As demonstrated in this book, NLP techniques offer a strategic advantage in various professional settings, enabling individuals to communicate more persuasively, resolve conflicts more effectively, and achieve their career goals with greater success. Ultimately, incorporating NLP techniques into one's professional repertoire can lead to enhanced leadership capabilities and increased opportunities for advancement in the workplace.

Role of NLP in professional growth

The application of NLP in professional growth offers a myriad of benefits for individuals seeking to enhance their communication skills and overall effectiveness in the workplace. By understanding the principles of NLP such as calibration, anchoring, and reframing, professionals can develop a deeper awareness of both their own communication patterns and those of others. This heightened level of awareness allows individuals to build stronger rapport, influence others positively, and navigate complex interpersonal dynamics with greater ease. Through the use of NLP techniques, professionals can improve their ability to read verbal and non-verbal cues, tailor their communication style to suit different audiences, and resolve conflicts more effectively. Ultimately, embracing NLP in professional growth can lead to more successful interactions, improved leadership capabilities, and enhanced overall career advancement.

Case studies of career success facilitated by NLP

Throughout the chapters of "Decoding NLP", compelling case studies of career success facilitated by NLP provide concrete evidence of the effectiveness of these techniques in enhancing communication and achieving goals. For instance, one case study highlights a corporate executive who used NLP strategies to build rapport with his team, resulting in increased productivity and employee satisfaction. Another example showcases a therapist utilizing NLP to help clients overcome limiting beliefs and develop a more positive mindset, leading to transformative personal growth. These real-world examples demonstrate how NLP can empower individuals to navigate complex professional and personal dynamics with greater ease and success. By examining these case studies, readers gain valuable insights into the practical application of NLP principles, inspiring them to consider how these techniques can be leveraged to enhance their own careers and relationships.

XLIV. NLP AND AGING

As individuals age, their communication skills may undergo changes that can impact their relationships and overall well-being. NLP offers a promising avenue for addressing these challenges, providing tools and strategies to enhance communication effectiveness in the context of aging. By understanding how language, thoughts, and behaviors are interconnected, older adults can learn to adapt their communication styles to better connect with others and convey their needs and desires clearly. Additionally, NLP techniques such as mirroring, pacing, and leading can help older individuals build rapport and establish trust with those around them, leading to more meaningful interactions and improved social connections. As the population continues to age, the integration of NLP principles into programs and interventions aimed at supporting older adults could have profound benefits for their psychological well-being and quality of life.

Application of NLP in gerontology

NLP has gained recognition in the field of gerontology as a valuable tool for enhancing communication and improving the quality of care for elderly individuals. By incorporating NLP techniques into interactions with older adults, caregivers and healthcare professionals can better understand their unique needs and preferences, establish rapport more effectively, and address emotional and psychological aspects of aging. Through techniques such as mirroring, pacing, and leading, practitioners can create a positive and supportive environment that fosters trust and connection with elderly patients. NLP also offers strategies for managing challenging behaviors, addressing cognitive decline, and promoting overall well-being in older adults. By applying NLP principles in gerontological care, professionals can transform the way they communicate and ultimately enhance the quality of life for elderly individuals.

NLP techniques for enhancing life quality in aging

Within the realm of aging and life quality improvement, the utilization of NLP techniques stands as a promising avenue for enhancing overall well-being. As individuals age, they may encounter various challenges that impact their mental, emotional, and physical health. By incorporating NLP principles such as reframing negative thoughts, anchoring positive emotions, and enhancing communication skills, older adults can experience a profound shift in their perception of aging. Through the practice of NLP, individuals can learn to reframe limiting beliefs about aging, cultivate a more positive outlook on life, and strengthen their relationships with others. Additionally, NLP techniques can help older individuals establish a sense of empowerment and agency, enabling them to navigate life transitions with resilience and purpose. By integrating NLP practices into aging-related interventions, professionals in the field can effectively support older adults in preserving their quality of life and promoting holistic well-being as they age.

Case studies of NLP applications in elder care

As the field of elder care continues to evolve, the integration of NLP has shown promising results in improving communication and overall well-being for elderly individuals. Case studies have highlighted the benefits of applying NLP techniques in elder care settings, where practitioners have utilized strategies such as mirroring and matching to establish rapport with seniors with cognitive impairments. By using language patterns and sensory-based cues, caregivers have been able to understand the unique needs and preferences of elderly individuals, enhancing the quality of their interactions and fostering a sense of connection. These studies reveal the transformative power of NLP in enhancing communication with older adults, ultimately improving their emotional health and quality of life. The application of NLP in elder care not only demonstrates its practical utility but also underscores its potential to positively impact the lives of vulnerable populations in need of effective communication strategies.

XLV. NLP AND PARENTING

NLP techniques can be particularly beneficial when applied to the realm of parenting. By utilizing NLP concepts such as anchoring and reframing, parents can enhance their communication with their children, leading to improved understanding, cooperation, and emotional connection. For instance, by anchoring positive emotions to specific behaviors or experiences, parents can reinforce desired behaviors in their children, creating a more harmonious and constructive family dynamic. Additionally, reframing challenging situations can help parents and children see things from different perspectives, fostering empathy and resilience. By incorporating NLP principles into their parenting approach, caregivers can cultivate a nurturing environment that promotes mutual understanding and growth. Ultimately, NLP offers parents a valuable toolkit to navigate the complexities of family dynamics and foster strong, healthy relationships with their children.

Enhancing parenting skills through NLP

By integrating NLP techniques into parenting practices, caregivers can significantly enhance their skills and create a more harmonious and effective relationship with their children. NLP offers tools and strategies for improved communication, understanding, and connection with the younger generation. Through techniques such as mirroring, pacing, and leading, parents can better attune themselves to their child's needs and emotions, leading to a deeper level of empathy and understanding. Additionally, the concept of anchoring can assist parents in creating positive associations and behaviors within their children, reinforcing desirable actions and responses. By learning and utilizing these NLP strategies, parents can cultivate a supportive and nurturing environment that promotes healthy development and growth in their children. Ultimately, enhancing parenting skills through NLP can lead to stronger bonds, improved communication, and more positive outcomes for both parents and their children.

NLP strategies for effective communication with children

An essential aspect of utilizing NLP in effective communication with children is the adoption of strategies that cater to their unique needs and developmental stages. Firstly, it is crucial to establish a strong rapport based on trust and understanding, allowing the child to feel safe and valued in the interaction. Utilizing NLP techniques such as mirroring and matching can help establish a connection with the child by reflecting their body language and speech patterns. Secondly, employing anchoring techniques can assist in creating positive associations with certain behaviors or emotions, reinforcing desired behaviors in children through consistent reinforcement. Finally, utilizing reframing strategies can help shift the child's perspective on challenging situations, fostering a more positive and growth-oriented mindset. By incorporating these NLP strategies tailored to children's communication styles and perspectives, adults can effectively engage with young individuals, promote effective understanding, and build stronger relationships based on mutual respect and empathy.

Examples of improved family dynamics using NLP

A powerful example of improved family dynamics using NLP can be seen in the case of a family struggling with constant conflicts and misunderstandings. By incorporating NLP techniques such as reframing and rapport building, family members were able to shift their perspectives and communicate more effectively. Through guided exercises and reflective discussions, parents and children alike learned to understand each other's communication styles and emotional triggers, leading to a more harmonious and supportive family environment. Furthermore, by utilizing anchoring techniques to create positive associations and outcomes, the family experienced a transformation in their interactions, fostering greater empathy and cooperation. In this way, NLP provided the tools and strategies necessary for the family to navigate challenging situations with empathy and understanding, ultimately strengthening their bond and creating a more cohesive and nurturing family dynamic.

XLVI. NLP AND ADDICTION RECOVERY

One area where NLP has shown significant promise is in addiction recovery. By understanding the language patterns and belief systems that contribute to addictive behaviors, individuals can begin to unravel the root causes of their addictions and develop healthier coping mechanisms. Through techniques like reframing, individuals can shift their perspectives on addiction, viewing it as a challenge to overcome rather than a permanent state of being. Anchoring techniques can also be employed to help individuals create positive associations with sobriety, making it easier to resist cravings and triggers. By incorporating NLP into addiction recovery programs, therapists and individuals alike can work towards breaking the cycle of addiction and building a more stable foundation for long-term sobriety. This holistic approach to recovery addresses not only the physical aspects of addiction but also the psychological and emotional components, leading to more comprehensive and lasting results.

Role of NLP in addiction treatment

NLP has demonstrated significant potential in addiction treatment by enhancing communication between therapists and patients. Through NLP techniques such as reframing and anchoring, therapists can effectively address underlying beliefs and behaviors that contribute to addiction. By helping individuals reframe their thoughts and emotions surrounding substance use, NLP can promote healthier coping mechanisms and reduce the likelihood of relapse. Moreover, NLP can improve rapport between therapists and clients, fostering a supportive and trusting environment crucial for successful treatment outcomes. By utilizing NLP in addiction therapy, therapists can empower individuals to overcome addictive patterns and achieve long-term recovery. The integration of NLP into addiction treatment not only enhances communication but also provides a new avenue for exploring the psychological roots of addiction and facilitating lasting change.

NLP techniques for overcoming addictive behaviors

NLP techniques have shown promise in assisting individuals in overcoming addictive behaviors through various strategies. By utilizing techniques such as reframing, individuals can change their perspectives on addictive behaviors, shifting their mindset from one of dependency to one of empowerment. Anchoring techniques are also effective in breaking the cycle of addictive behaviors by associating negative emotions with the behavior, thereby reducing the desire to engage in such actions. Additionally, NLP techniques can help individuals understand the underlying triggers of their addictive behaviors, allowing them to address the root causes effectively. Through a combination of NLP techniques, individuals can develop new coping mechanisms, reprogram their thought patterns, and establish healthier habits, paving the way towards lasting recovery and a fulfilling, addiction-free life.

Success stories of addiction recovery using NLP

One notable success story in addiction recovery using NLP involves a middle-aged man struggling with a long history of substance abuse. Through NLP techniques such as reframing negative beliefs and anchoring positive emotions, this individual was able to break free from his destructive behavior patterns and develop healthier coping mechanisms. By working with a skilled practitioner, he learned to recognize triggers, reprogram his thought patterns, and build resilience against relapse. As a result, he experienced a significant improvement in his overall well-being, reported reduced cravings, and achieved long-term sobriety. This case exemplifies the power of NLP in facilitating transformative change and providing individuals with the tools needed to overcome addiction and thrive in recovery. Through targeted interventions and personalized strategies, NLP can offer hope and support to those struggling with addiction, paving the way for lasting healing and success.

XLVII. NLP AND EXECUTIVE COACHING

In the realm of executive coaching, NLP has emerged as a powerful tool for enhancing leadership effectiveness and communication skills. By utilizing NLP techniques, executive coaches can help leaders develop a deeper understanding of their own communication styles and how they impact their relationships with team members and stakeholders. Through the exploration of NLP concepts such as perceptual positions, meta-modeling, and sensory acuity, coaches can facilitate transformative shifts in their clients' communication patterns. By integrating NLP into executive coaching sessions, coaches can empower leaders to improve their ability to influence and inspire others, navigate challenging conversations, and build stronger relationships based on trust and empathy. Ultimately, the incorporation of NLP principles into executive coaching practices can lead to enhanced leadership performance and organizational success.

NLP's impact on executive performance

One significant area where NLP has shown its impact is in enhancing executive performance. By understanding and applying NLP techniques, executives can improve their communication skills, build stronger relationships, and lead more effectively. Through techniques such as calibration, anchoring, and reframing, executives can better interpret verbal and non-verbal cues, establish rapport with their teams, and influence outcomes positively. Case studies and examples in the field demonstrate how NLP has helped leaders overcome barriers to communication and achieve their goals in various professional settings. By adopting a more mindful and strategic communication approach, executives can navigate complex situations with confidence and clarity. Ultimately, incorporating NLP into their toolkit can lead to increased productivity, improved team dynamics, and overall organizational success. This highlights the importance of NLP in empowering executives to perform at their best in today's competitive business landscape.

Techniques for executive coaching using NLP

In the realm of executive coaching, NLP offers a powerful set of techniques for fostering personal and professional growth. One key method involves utilizing NLP to enhance communication skills, enabling executives to better connect with their teams, peers, and stakeholders. By honing their ability to understand and influence both verbal and non-verbal cues, executives can build rapport more effectively and navigate complex interpersonal dynamics with greater finesse. Techniques such as calibration allow executives to attune themselves to the emotions and behaviors of others, while anchoring provides a way to associate positive experiences with desired outcomes. Additionally, reframing enables executives to reframe challenges as opportunities, fostering a more optimistic and solution-oriented mindset. Overall, by incorporating NLP techniques into executive coaching, individuals can develop a more nuanced and impactful communication style that drives success and fosters strong relationships within the workplace.

Case studies of executive improvement through NLP

As demonstrated in various case studies, executive improvement through NLP has shown remarkable success in enhancing leadership skills and communication effectiveness. For instance, a study focusing on a CEO who underwent NLP training revealed significant improvements in decision-making, conflict resolution, and team collaboration. By utilizing NLP techniques such as modeling successful behaviors, setting powerful goals, and enhancing sensory acuity, the executive was able to cultivate a more dynamic and influential leadership style. Another case study showcased how a senior manager utilized NLP strategies to boost employee engagement, foster creativity, and increase team productivity. These examples highlight the transformative impact of NLP on executive performance, emphasizing the importance of integrating such tools into leadership development programs for maximizing professional growth and organizational success.

XLVIII. NLP AND MEDIA COMMUNICATION

In the realm of media communication, NLP offers a powerful toolkit for enhancing the way individuals interact and engage with various forms of media. By understanding the intricate connections between language, behavior, and thought patterns, individuals can decipher the underlying messages embedded in media content more effectively. NLP techniques such as modeling, mirroring, and pacing can help individuals establish rapport with media consumers, tailor messages to resonate with specific audiences, and ultimately shape perceptions and influence behaviors. When applied thoughtfully, NLP can not only optimize the impact of media messages but also foster deeper connections and engagement with audiences. As technology continues to evolve, the integration of NLP principles into media communication strategies will undoubtedly play a pivotal role in shaping the future of media interactions and storytelling.

Adapting NLP for media professionals

Within the realm of media professionals, the adaptation of NLP techniques can prove to be a powerful tool for enhancing communication effectiveness. By utilizing NLP principles, including sensory acuity, language patterns, and perceptual positions, media professionals can better understand their audience's needs and tailor their messaging accordingly. Through the practice of calibration, media professionals can finely tune their delivery to resonate with viewers or readers on a deeper level, ultimately increasing engagement and impact. Additionally, anchoring techniques can be employed to evoke specific emotions or responses, strategically influencing viewer perception. Furthermore, by mastering the art of reframing, media professionals can shift perspectives and reposition narratives to craft more compelling and persuasive content. By integrating NLP strategies into their repertoire, media professionals can elevate their communication skills, foster stronger connections with their audience, and ultimately achieve greater success in their field.

Techniques for effective communication in media

In the realm of effective communication in media, numerous techniques can be employed to ensure clarity, engagement, and impact. One prominent method is the use of storytelling to convey complex messages in a compelling and relatable manner. By weaving narratives that resonate with the audience, media professionals can capture attention, evoke emotions, and drive home key points effectively. Moreover, leveraging visual aids such as infographics, videos, and multimedia presentations can enhance the understanding and retention of information. These tools provide a dynamic and engaging way to communicate complex ideas, making them more accessible to a wide audience. Additionally, active listening and empathy are essential skills for effective communication in media, allowing communicators to better understand their audience's perspective and tailor their message accordingly. By combining storytelling, visual aids, and empathetic listening, media professionals can create impactful and resonant communication that leaves a lasting impression on their audience.

Examples of NLP in journalism and broadcasting

One compelling example of NLP in journalism and broadcasting is the use of anchoring techniques to influence audience perception. By strategically linking certain words or images with specific emotions or beliefs, journalists and broadcasters can subtly shape the way their audience interprets information. For instance, a news anchor may use anchoring to associate a particular political figure with positive or negative connotations, influencing how viewers perceive that individual. Additionally, reframing techniques can be employed to shift the focus of a story or conversation, steering it in a direction that aligns with a certain agenda. By understanding and utilizing these NLP tools, journalists and broadcasters can effectively control the narrative and frame discussions in a way that serves their desired outcomes. Through careful application of NLP principles, communication professionals can skillfully guide audience perceptions and ultimately shape public opinion.

XLIX. NLP AND ENVIRONMENTAL COMMUNICATION

As the field of environmental communication continues to grow, the integration of NLP techniques offers a unique approach to enhancing communication strategies. By leveraging NLP principles such as modeling, meta-programs, and representational systems, environmental communicators can better understand the perspectives and values of different stakeholders, thus fostering more meaningful dialogues around pressing environmental issues. NLP can also be instrumental in crafting messages that are tailored to resonate with specific audience segments, leading to increased engagement and receptiveness to environmental initiatives. Furthermore, by utilizing NLP tools like sensory acuity and language patterns, communicators can effectively convey complex scientific information in a manner that is easily digestible and compelling for diverse audiences. By incorporating NLP into environmental communication practices, professionals in the field can elevate the impact of their messages and catalyze positive behavioral change towards sustainable practices.

Using NLP to promote environmental awareness

In today's world, as environmental issues continue to gain prominence, the need for effective communication strategies to promote environmental awareness has never been more crucial. NLP offers a powerful tool for achieving this goal by enhancing individuals' ability to both receive and transmit messages in a compelling and persuasive manner. Through the application of

NLP techniques such as reframing and anchoring, individuals can tailor their communication style to resonate with varied audiences, making complex environmental issues more accessible and engaging. By fostering a deeper connection with their audience, communicators can inspire action and promote environmental stewardship more effectively. NLP can help bridge the gap between scientific information and public engagement, enabling a more informed and environmentally conscious society. Embracing NLP in the realm of environmental communication has the potential to drive real change by fostering a greater sense of connectedness and responsibility towards our planet.

NLP strategies for effective environmental advocacy

In the realm of environmental advocacy, employing NLP strategies can significantly enhance communication effectiveness. By utilizing techniques such as calibration, anchoring, and reframing, advocates can tailor their messages to resonate with diverse audiences, thereby increasing receptivity to environmental issues. Through NLP, individuals can better understand the underlying motivations and beliefs of their audience, allowing them to craft persuasive arguments that address specific concerns and values. Furthermore, NLP techniques can aid in building rapport and establishing trust, essential components for influencing behavior change and inspiring action. By incorporating NLP into their advocacy efforts, environmentalists can foster meaningful connections with stakeholders, mobilize support for sustainability initiatives, and ultimately drive positive change for the planet. This strategic application of NLP positions environmental advocates as effective communicators who can successfully convey the importance of environmental protection to a wide range of audiences.

Case studies of environmental campaigns using NLP

The application of NLP in environmental campaigns has yielded promising results, as evidenced by various case studies. One such example is a campaign focused on reducing plastic pollution in oceans, where NLP techniques were used to craft compelling messaging that resonated with the target audience's values and emotions. By carefully calibrating language and visual cues, the campaign was able to anchor a sense of urgency and responsibility in the viewers, ultimately leading to increased awareness and behavioral change. Furthermore, by reframing the issue of plastic pollution as a threat to marine biodiversity and human health, the campaign successfully motivated individuals to take action and support sustainable practices. These case studies highlight the power of NLP in shaping public perception and behavior towards environmental issues, making it a valuable tool for communication and advocacy in the field of sustainability.

L. NLP AND ARTIFICIAL INTELLIGENCE

NLP is closely intertwined with AI in its quest to enhance communication effectiveness. By utilizing AI algorithms, NLP can analyze large datasets of text to discern patterns and trends in language usage, allowing for the development of more sophisticated techniques. This marriage of NLP and AI has the potential to revolutionize the way we understand and utilize language, providing deeper insights into human communication patterns and behaviors. The synergy between NLP and AI has already shown promising results in various fields, from customer service chatbots to sentiment analysis in social media. As technology continues to advance, the integration of NLP and AI will play a crucial role in shaping the future of communication, paving the way for more personalized and efficient interactions across diverse contexts.

Integration of NLP techniques with AI technology

The integration of NLP techniques with AI technology represents a powerful synergy that can revolutionize the way we communicate and interact in the digital age. By combining the insights of NLP, which focuses on understanding the interplay between language, behavior, and thought patterns, with the capabilities of AI to process vast amounts of data and derive meaningful insights, we can unlock new possibilities for enhancing human-machine interactions. This fusion enables AI systems to engage in more natural and contextually relevant conversations, adapt to users' emotional states, and personalize responses in a way that mimics human empathy. By leveraging NLP techniques within AI technology, we can create more intuitive interfaces, improve decision-making processes, and enhance overall user experience. This innovative approach has the potential to drive significant advancements in various fields, from customer service and healthcare to education and entertainment, ultimately reshaping the way we communicate and connect in a technology-driven world.

Potential impacts of AI on NLP practices

The integration of AI into NLP practices has the potential to revolutionize the way we communicate and interact with technology. AI-powered NLP systems can analyze vast amounts of textual data at incredible speeds, extracting valuable insights and patterns that can be used to enhance various communication processes. By leveraging machine learning algorithms, these systems can continually improve their language understanding capabilities, enabling more accurate sentiment analysis, language translation, and semantic understanding. Moreover, AI-driven NLP tools can assist in automating tasks such as language generation, information extraction, and text summarization, streamlining communication workflows and increasing efficiency. However, as with any technological advancement, there are potential ethical considerations to be mindful of, such as data privacy, algorithmic bias, and the impact on human labor. It is imperative for researchers, developers, and policymakers to carefully navigate these complexities to ensure that AI-enhanced NLP practices are deployed responsibly and ethically.

Future prospects of NLP and AI collaboration

The future prospects of collaboration between NLP and AI hold immense potential for revolutionizing various fields. As AI continues to advance, integrating NLP capabilities can enhance the understanding and processing of human language, leading to more sophisticated conversational AI systems and improved natural language understanding. By leveraging NLP techniques such as sentiment analysis, text summarization, and language translation, AI systems can become more adept at extracting insights from vast amounts of textual data, making them invaluable in sectors like healthcare, finance, marketing, and customer service. Furthermore, the synergy between NLP and AI can pave the way for more personalized and interactive user experiences, driving innovation in virtual assistants, chatbots, and automated language processing systems. With ongoing research and development in this domain, the collaboration between NLP and AI is poised to redefine the way we communicate, interact, and engage with technology in the coming years.

LI. CONCLUSION

In conclusion, the exploration of NLP in this book reveals its profound potential to revolutionize communication practices. By delving into techniques such as calibration, anchoring, and reframing, individuals can cultivate a deep understanding of verbal and non-verbal cues, establish strong rapport, and effectively influence others. Through engaging case studies and practical examples, the application of NLP tools by various professionals underscores their versatility and efficacy in overcoming communication barriers and achieving desired outcomes. Moreover, the invitation to self-reflect on one's communication style and embrace a more conscious approach underscores the transformative impact of NLP on interpersonal dynamics. As a comprehensive resource for enhancing communication skills and fostering stronger relationships, "Decoding NLP" serves as a valuable guide for individuals seeking to unlock their full communicative potential and navigate interactions with clarity and purpose.

Summary of key findings

The key findings of this research on NLP reveal its profound impact on enhancing communication skills in various contexts. Through examining concepts such as calibration, anchoring, and reframing, it becomes evident how these techniques can be effectively utilized to decipher verbal and non-verbal cues, establish strong rapport, and influence others positively. Case studies and practical examples presented throughout the book highlight the real-world application of NLP tools in overcoming communication hurdles and achieving desired outcomes. By encouraging readers to reflect on their communication styles and adopt a more mindful approach, this research not only equips individuals with practical strategies but also promotes personal growth and self-awareness. Through the exploration of NLP, this study underscores the transformative potential of improved communication in fostering fulfilling interpersonal relationships and achieving professional success.

Implications of NLP for future communication practices

In the realm of communication practices, the implications of NLP for the future are profound and far-reaching. As individuals continue to seek ways to enhance their understanding of others and effectively convey their messages, the principles of NLP provide a valuable framework. By mastering techniques such as calibration, anchoring, and reframing, individuals can better navigate complex social interactions and influence outcomes positively. These tools not only offer practical applications in professional settings but also hold significant promise for improving personal relationships and self-awareness. As the field of NLP continues to evolve and gain recognition, its role in shaping future communication practices cannot be understated. By fostering a more holistic and mindful approach to communication, NLP has the potential to transform the way individuals engage with others, leading to more meaningful connections and successful outcomes.

Final thoughts on the power of NLP in enhancing communication skills

As we reflect on the power of NLP in enhancing communication skills, it becomes evident that this approach offers a multifaceted toolkit for individuals seeking to elevate their interactions. By delving into concepts such as calibration, anchoring, and reframing, individuals can gain a deeper understanding of how to effectively convey their messages and interpret the signals of others. Through the use of NLP techniques, individuals can build stronger rapport, influence others positively, and navigate through complex communication scenarios with ease. The practical examples and case studies presented in this book showcase real-world applications of NLP in various contexts, highlighting its versatility and effectiveness. Ultimately, by adopting NLP principles, individuals can not only improve their communication skills but also foster more meaningful connections and achieve their desired outcomes in both personal and professional settings.

BIBLIOGRAPHY

Johan Coetsee. 'Change Lessons from the CEO.' Real People, Real Change, Patrick C. Flood, John Wiley & Sons, 11/18/2013

Michael J. Losier. 'Law of Connection.' The Science of Using NLP to Create Ideal Personal and Professional Relationships, Grand Central Publishing, 6/1/2009

Lynne Cooper. 'Business NLP For Dummies, UK Edition.' John Wiley & Sons, 3/23/2011

Camilla Gyllensvan. 'NLP Communication & Conscious Leadership.' Train Your Brain to Top Performance, Mindboozt Publications, 5/29/2018

Rex Morton. 'The Impact of NLP Techniques on Conflict Resolution and Negotiation Skills.' Amazon Digital Services LLC - Kdp, 11/11/2023

Thomas M. Holtgraves. 'The Oxford Handbook of Language and Social Psychology.' Oxford University Press, 9/2/2014

Herb Bisno. 'Managing Conflict.' SAGE Publications, 1/1/1988

Mary Catherine Stewart. 'Tools for Conflict Resolution.' A Practical K-12 Program Based on Peter Senge's 5th Discipline, Ellen M. O'Keefe, R&L Education, 1/1/2004

Shawnee Giessinger. 'Cognitive Reframing: How to Live More Positively.' Reframing Techniques, Independently Published, 4/4/2021

John Grinder. 'Reframing.' Neuro-linguistic Programming [Trade Mark Symbol] and the Transformation of Meaning, Richard Bandler, Real People Press, 1/1/1982

Dennis K. Mumby. 'Reframing Difference in Organizational Communication Studies.' Research, Pedagogy, and Practice, SAGE, 1/1/2011

United States. Federal Aviation Administration. 'Special Military Operations.' U.S. Department of Transportation, Federal Aviation Administration, 1/1/1990

Harry B. Lancelot. 'Anchors in Concrete--design and Behavior.' George A. Senkiw, Harry B. Lancelot III, Editors, George A. Senkiw, American Concrete Institute, 1/1/1991

Tom Dotz. 'NLP.' The Essential Guide to Neuro-Linguistic Programming, Tom Hoobyar, Harper Collins, 2/12/2013

Christoph Molnar. 'Interpretable Machine Learning.' Lulu.com, 1/1/2020

Charles C. Poirier. 'Using Models to Improve the Supply Chain.' CRC Press, 8/26/2003

John White. 'The Routledge Dictionary of Nonverbal Communication.' David B. Givens, Routledge, 5/26/2021

Jay L. Bucher. 'The Quality Calibration Handbook.' Developing and Managing a Calibration Program, Quality Press, 7/26/2006

United States. Department of the Army. 'Calibration Specialist.' [Department of Defense], Department of the Army, Headquarters, 1/1/1979

NARAYAN CHANGDER. 'THE GIRL WHO LOVED SPIDERS.' Changder Outline, 11/27/2023

Jay A. Conger. 'The Necessary Art of Persuasion.' Harvard Business Review Press, 9/8/2008

Bryan Westra. 'The Essential Milton Model And Meta Model Learnings.' Direct And Indirect Forms Of Communication So You Can Change Minds And Persuasions Without A Question Or Doubt, Confidently, CreateSpace Independent Publishing Platform, 6/7/2015

Janis Hostad. 'Illuminating the Diversity of Cancer and Palliative Care Education.' A Complete Resource for EMQs & a Complete Resource for MCQs, Volume 1 & 2, Lorna Foyle, CRC Press, 4/19/2018

Martin Gogolla. 'Theory and Practice of Model Transformations.' Third International Conference, ICMT 2010, Malaga, Spain, June 28-July 2, 2010. Proceedings, Laurence Tratt, Springer, 6/29/2010

Douglas R. Long. 'Electronic cryptographic communications equipment specialist (AFSC 30650)..' John M. Hardy, Extension Course Institute, Air University, 1/1/1985

M. Tamer Özsu. 'Encyclopedia of Database Systems.' Ling Liu, Springer New York, 1/1/2019

Pierre J. (Pierre Joseph) Gelinas. 'The NLP Meta-model and Psychological Adjustment [microform].' Thesis (M.Ed.)--University of Alberta, 1/1/1982

Neville F. Hacker. 'Berek and Hacker's Gynecologic Oncology.' Jonathan S. Berek, Lippincott Williams & Wilkins, 1/1/2010

Mark Benedict. 'The Method of Selling.' Your Key to Successful Sales with Over 70 Creative Selling Techniques, The Method of Selling, 6/1/2007

Brian Icenhower. 'The High-Performing Real Estate Team.' 5 Keys to Dramatically Increasing Sales and Commissions, John Wiley & Sons, 9/21/2021

Kate Burton. 'Building Rapport with NLP In A Day For Dummies.' Romilla Ready, John Wiley & Sons, 5/25/2012

Wilson Learning Corporation. 'Communication Styles.' Wilson Learning Corporation, 1/1/1999

Alan Thomas "Chip." Mattar. 'Primary Representational Systems as a Basis for Improved Comprehension and Communication.' Utah State University. Department of Psychology, 1/1/1980

Bradley W. Kuhns, Ph.D., O.M.D.. 'Mind/Body Theray, Auditory, Visual,Kinesthetic, (NLP).' Bradley Kuhns,Ph.D.,O.M.D., 1/1/2010

Bodo Winter. 'Sensory Linguistics.' Language, perception and metaphor, John Benjamins Publishing Company, 4/24/2019

Monica Hanaway. 'Existential Perspectives on Coaching.' Emmy van Deurzen, Bloomsbury Publishing, 4/20/2012

Charles V.W. Brooks. 'Reclaiming Vitality and Presence.' Sensory Awareness as a Practice for Life, Charlotte Selver, North Atlantic Books, 4/24/2007

Eduardo D Rodriguez. 'Facial Trauma Surgery E-Book.' From Primary Repair to Reconstruction, Amir H Dorafshar, Elsevier Health Sciences, 2/18/2019

Joseph P. Forgas. 'The Message Within.' The Role of Subjective Experience In Social Cognition And Behavior, Herbert Bless, Psychology Press, 12/19/2013

Dr Tim Brunson. 'Mastering the NLP Communication Model.' Independently Published, 7/21/2021

Mohamed El Mahfoudi. 'Nlp.' How to Use Neuro Linguistic Programming Presuppositions to Break Free from Limiting Beliefs, Independently Published, 8/23/2020

Joseph O'Connor. 'NLP.' Thorsons, 1/1/2001

John Grinder. 'The Origins Of Neuro Linguistic Programming.' Crown House Publishing, 5/9/2013

Ajay Uppili Arasanipalai. 'Applied Natural Language Processing in the Enterprise.' Ankur A. Patel, "O'Reilly Media, Inc.", 5/12/2021

Diana Ridley. 'The Literature Review.' A Step-by-Step Guide for Students, SAGE, 7/23/2012

Sally Dimmick. 'Successful Communication Through NLP.' A Trainer's Guide, Gower Publishing, Ltd., 1/1/1995

Barbara Gibson. 'The Complete Guide to Understanding and Using NLP.' Neuro-linguistic Programming Explained Simply, Atlantic Publishing Company, 1/1/2011

Alistair McCleery. 'An Introduction to Book History.' David Finkelstein, Routledge, 3/13/2006

9 798326 076977